*To my wife, Kim,
and to all who encouraged me
to put my thoughts on paper*

ROMANS

The Foundational Truths of Romans 1-8

Written by Bob Warren

ISBN: 978-1-62727-000-7

Cover design by Dan Carter

Table of Contents

Introduction

Do you know Christ? I mean, do you know Him as your friend, your companion, your life? Do those around you desire what you have in Jesus? Do you see each day as an opportunity to display the character and love of the Savior, even when you don't feel like it? If you waivered on your answer to any of these questions, a study of Romans 1-8 may be just what you need.

This course covers Romans 1-8, which may be the most important section of the entire Word of God. No portion of Scripture has marked my life like these eight chapters. Your time in this book should: (1) Result in a deeper understanding of Christ's sacrifice on the cross (2) Give you a greater desire to love Him with all of your heart. After all, *"faith"* can work effectively only *"through love"* (Galatians 5:6).

> *For in Christ Jesus neither circumcision nor uncircumcision means anything, but*
> *faith working through love.* (Galatians 5:6)

Recently, while teaching on the subject of faith, I asked the class if the faith required prior to salvation originates with man or with God. Much to my surprise, many of the students answered, "with God." Some of them had completed the original *Romans 1-8* study, so I instantly realized the need to expand my commentary on the subject in this present edition. For instance, I wrote on page 34 of the original *Romans 1-8* study: "Several years ago I saw my need for a Savior. When this occurred, I just basically made a choice to look up, and God did all the rest. He (at that moment) granted me repentance (2Timothy 2:25; Acts 11:18), gave me faith (Romans 12:3), and then justified me." I have been intrigued by the number of students who, as a result of these words, have misunderstood my beliefs regarding repentance and faith. If you are one of those students, I apologize for not writing more concerning these subjects in that original work. I just assumed that the statements, "Several years ago I saw my need for a Savior" and "When this occurred, I just basically made a choice to look up, and God did all the rest," communicated that the faith I exercised prior to spiritual regeneration (and while depraved) originated with me. I assumed, evidently incorrectly, that the words, "saw my need for a Savior," validated that I exercised repentance, and that the statement, "made a choice to look up," verified that faith was exercised—and that both repentance and faith were exercised in my depravity prior to receiving God's salvation.

No doubt, we were granted *"...a measure of faith"* (Romans 12:3) once we were made new in Christ subsequent to repenting and believing while depraved. However, this is not the same faith that God requires from the depraved prior to placing them in His Son. This subject is covered in much depth in Week 7 of the course. Consequently, if any confusion remains, know that help is on the horizon. By the way, the term "depravity" points to our lost state before we were spiritually regenerated. In other words, *to be depraved* means to be lost and separated from God. However, the depraved are capable of exercising repentance and faith prior to spiritual regeneration, as will be validated later. Remember this as we continue, for the terms "depravity" and "depraved" are used throughout the study.

*R*omans 1-8 may be the most important section of the entire Word of God.

If you should be interested, I have written a work titled *God's Heart: As it Relates to Depravity,* a work that addresses this subject in great detail.

If you have been introduced to this course at a previous date, you will note that revisions have been made throughout this text. They are present due to the theological shift that has occurred within Christendom since the earlier writing. Much can change in twenty years, and it has. Yes, a theological alteration has occurred to the confusion of many. Therefore, several subjects mentioned only briefly in the original *Romans 1-8* course are addressed more thoroughly in this present study. The goal is for every reader to understand exactly what is being communicated, a challenge indeed considering the overabundance of theological ideas flooding Christendom today.

I no longer teach assuming that the listener's definition of a theological term is equivalent to mine. Our present postmodern era which denies absolutes and disregards contradictions dictates this behavior. When a system, regardless of its label, redefines words for the sake of preserving a preconceived notion, the system has become more valuable than the truth. Hence pragmatism takes precedence over truth, and truth takes a backseat to man's ideology. When pragmatism rules, the system which is billed as producing life produces agonizing death. This tragedy is occurring in our day, even within the confines of Christianity. Therefore, our only hope is to know truth based on its context, allowing definitions to remain as they were when God penned His infallible letter to man.

As a teacher, I owe it to you to hide none of what I believe regarding the Creator and His Word. Consequently, my heart and soul are not only embedded in the confines of this work, but are laid bare before you as well. My policy is to speak and write exactly what I deem to be the truth—even though some, maybe many, might disagree. This mindset has served me well over the years, so I trust you will enjoy what follows.

These days we must define specifically what we mean while using certain theological terminology. This necessity is due to the above-mentioned shift in the theological environment of our day. For instance, the word "salvation" may mean one thing to you and something totally different to someone else. The same applies to "faith," or "forgiveness," or your "identity" in Christ. These terms are many times tossed about as though they are perceived identically by all believers. Because they are no longer universally understood, this revised version of *Romans 1-8* was birthed.

I have written from a no-holes-barred frame of reference. In other words, I have written assuming that: (1) The reader knows nothing regarding the subject matter or (2) The reader has attached a totally different meaning to the terms involved. Any person, regardless of the level of spiritual maturity, can, therefore, benefit from this revised work, even if in disagreement with its conclusions. After all, if we are confident in what we believe, we should welcome any argument against what we deem to be the truth. Otherwise, we have become unteachable, a dangerous condition indeed.

This course is easy to follow. Six days of each week you will read Scripture and answer a set of corresponding questions. Also included are lessons that should not only answer the questions, but tie together the entire week's study for easy reference. If you can't answer a particular question (after exhausting all resources), feel free to read the portion of the lesson that pertains to the question. The answer should be provided.

Taking the course with one or more persons is best (Ecclesiastes 4:9-12). Discussing what you learn with fellow students will stimulate growth and add an exciting dimension to the experience as well. Even so, if your only alternative is to go it alone, that will be fine. Just make sure to

Our only hope is to know truth based on its context.

hold yourself accountable for finishing what you have started. You can order the audio teaching sessions associated with this series online at www.lifeonthehill.org. You can also call 270-437-4172.

If you need additional copies of the course, we would appreciate your contacting us. We process and ship all requests in three to five business days. Because the proceeds from these materials help meet the needs of The Hill, we ask you to refrain from making your own copies. Thank you for honoring our request.

The course will be covered in 19 weeks. Six to seven weeks of study will be required to build a foundation to support the weighty truths of the remaining weeks. The truths in Romans 1-4 are essential, but the meat of the book is contained in Romans 5-8. If you don't have nineteen weeks to devote to the study, you may want to start with the questions located in Week 7 (Romans 5:1) and work from there. If you choose this route, make sure to read the lessons associated with Weeks 1-6 prior to starting Week 7. You can answer the questions associated with Weeks 1-6 at a later date.

Do you want to be free, I mean really free? Do you want to know what it means for Christ to live His life through you? Do you, like Paul, truly desire to *"know Him"* (Philippians 3:10)? If so, you have begun a journey that could yield such fruit. God Himself will change you, but we trust He will use this course as a tool through which to do His work.

Take time to read all Scripture references. You will be glad you did. Scripture text is taken from the New American Standard Bible (NASB) unless otherwise noted. If you do not have a copy of the New American Standard Bible, it might be wise to purchase one. I have used this version for years and have found it to be a wonderful resource for Biblical study. If obtaining a copy is not possible, use the version you have paying special attention to the NASB rendering of the passages addressed in the course. An advanced version of this study is also available, but it should be taken subsequent to the one you have in hand.

Romans 1 Questions

First Day

Ask the Lord to give you a supernatural ability to understand this week's lesson. Make sure to pray for wisdom (James 1:5).

Paul wrote the book of Romans in Corinth on his third missionary journey (Romans 16:23; 1Corinthians 1:14). He delivered the contribution mentioned in Romans 15:25-26 to Jerusalem at the end of his third journey. Evidently this letter was given to Phoebe, who was in Cenchrea, near Corinth, so she might deliver it to the church at Rome (Romans 16:1-2). Since Paul had not yet visited Rome, he addressed the fundamentals of the gospel in more detail in this epistle than in some of his others. In Romans, Paul not only defined the gospel, but explained its effect on those engaged in the adventure of faith.

1. Read Romans 1. In Romans 1:1, Paul refers to himself as a *"bond-servant."* According to Exodus 21:1-6 and Deuteronomy 15:12-17, what is a *"bond-servant"?* Why would Paul refer to himself in this manner?

2. Are you a bond-servant? If not, what changes will need to take place in your life before this transformation can become a reality?

3. To what is Paul referring in Romans 1:1when he uses the word *"gospel"?* (For assistance read 1Corinthians 15:1-8.)

4. Cross-referencing several of Paul's introductory statements in this epistle, how does Isaiah 53 tie in with Romans 1:2? How does Romans 1:3 relate to 1Chronicles 17:10-14?

5. How does Romans 1:4 tie in with 1Corinthians 15:12-19?

Second Day

1. Read Romans 1. According to Romans 1:7, *"Grace...and peace"* are available to man through a relationship with the *"Father"* and *"Jesus"* His Son. Why would Paul write *"Grace...and peace"* instead of peace and grace?

2.   After reading Romans 1:8, would you say that the church at Rome possessed great faith? Explain your answer. Could your friends make the same statement about you? If not, why not?

3.   What does Romans 1:9-10 communicate regarding Paul's prayer life and his concern for the believers at Rome? What would happen if the body of Christ prayed in a similar way for fellow believers? Pray today for each of your group members.

Third Day

1.   Read Romans 1. Why did Paul desire to visit the church at Rome (Romans 1:11-12)?

2.   According to Romans 1:12, what should happen when believers come together? Does it surprise you that Paul could be encouraged by those less mature than himself? Explain your answer.

3.   Had Paul visited Rome at the time of this writing? What verses provided your answer?

4.   To answer the following questions, refer to the latter portion of the book of Acts. Did Paul eventually visit Rome? If so, when, and under what circumstances?

Fourth Day

1.   Read Romans 1 and meditate on verses 16 and 17. Are you ever *"ashamed of the gospel"*? If so, when? What normally prompts this embarrassing response?

2.   How does Paul define *"the gospel"* in Romans 1:16? What does the gospel reveal (Romans 1:17)? What does Paul mean when he says, *"But the righteous man shall live by faith?"* This quote is from what book in the Old Testament?

Fifth Day

1. Read Romans 1. According to Romans 1:18, against what is *"the wrath of God...revealed"?*

2. Does everyone have an opportunity to know *"about God"* (Romans 1:19-20)? If so, through what avenue does this occur?

3. According to Romans 1:21-22, what happens to man when he refuses to *"honor"* God? How does this situation tie in with Proverbs 9:10?

4. How does Paul describe the behavior of a fool in Romans 1:23? When was the last time you observed someone exemplifying this type of behavior?

Sixth Day

1. Read Romans 1. What are the different stages that God gives man *"over to"* as man continues to reject His truth (Romans 1:24-32)?

2. With Paul's teaching in mind, what stage of rebellion is our society experiencing today? How does our present state tie in with Genesis 19:1-11? According to Genesis 19:12-26, how did God deal with the sin at Sodom? Doesn't this motivate you to carry the gospel to the world!?!

Romans 1 Lesson

Paul's Greeting

This first chapter is packed with a wealth of theological truths. We first learn that Paul generated this epistle (Romans 1:1) through the inspiration of the Holy Spirit and that he was a *"bond-servant"* of Christ. A *"bond-servant"* is one who has been set free by his master, but chooses to remain with and serve him for life (Exodus 21:5-6; Deuteronomy 15:12-17). This was Paul's perception of his relationship with the Lord. Jesus set Paul free! As a result of that freedom, Paul chose to submit to Christ forever. As we learn more about our freedom in Christ, we too will desire to become His bond-servants.

A *"bond-servant" is one who has been set free by his master, but chooses to remain with and serve him for life.*

Comprehending how Paul defines *"the gospel"* (Romans 1:1) is imperative. In 1Corinthians 15:1-8, we discover that the gospel refers to Jesus' death, burial, and resurrection. In Acts 1:11 and Hebrews 1:3, we learn that the gospel also includes the fact that Jesus is seated *"...at the right hand of the Majesty on high."* In Colossians 1:27 and Galatians 2:20, we understand that He now lives in every New Testament believer. What exciting news! What a wonderful gospel!

We need insight as to how these truths apply to our everyday experiences. Could it be that our Father desires that Christ live His life through us (since He lives in us), instead of us working <u>for</u> Him? That seems to make sense, especially since Christ is the only Person (He is also *"God"*— Hebrews 1:8) who has lived a sinless life.

Do you realize that the gospel was *"...promised beforehand through* [the] *prophets..."* (Romans 1:2)? Passages such as Isaiah 53 and Psalm 22 speak of a suffering Savior. In fact, much of the Old Testament points to Christ. These prophecies explain Paul's words in Romans 1:2:

> which was promised beforehand through His prophets in the holy Scriptures,
> (Romans 1:2)

Notice, too, that Paul uses the term *"holy"* when referring to the *"Scriptures."* No doubt existed in his mind as to the reliability and validity of what God had spoken. Do you view the Scriptures in this manner?

Paul mentions *"David"* in verse 3, for he (Paul) realized that Jesus was required to be a descendent of David to hold the office of Messiah. Why so? In 1Chronicles 17:11-14, we find that David was promised a descendent who would inherit an eternal throne. This descendent is the eternal Son of God, Jesus Christ. Being a descendent of David was not enough. Jesus' resurrection was the final proof of His Sonship and right to reign, as confirmed by 1Corinthians 15:12-19. Yes, Jesus *"...was declared the Son of God with power by the resurrection from the dead..."* (Romans 1:4). No wonder the resurrection has attracted so much attention for the past two thousand years.

Paul *"...received grace and apostleship..."* through Christ (Romans 1:5). Consequently, God's *"grace"* did more than save Paul <u>after</u> he exercised repentance and faith while depraved. God's *"grace"* also empowered Paul as he served as an apostle. This is verified by 1Corinthians 15:10:

> But by the grace of God I am what I am, and His grace toward me did not prove vain; but I labored even more than all of them, yet not I, but the grace of God with me. (1Corinthians 15:10)

If we choose to receive God's *"grace"* on a moment by moment basis, He will empower us as we take the good news of Christ to the world. Choosing to reject *"grace,"* however, causes us to drop out of the battle. Paul knew, beyond doubt, that he would be granted ample *"...grace...to bring about the obedience of faith among all the Gentiles..."* (Romans 1:5). The book of Acts verifies that this grace was abundantly supplied.

According to verse 7, all New Testament believers *"are beloved of God"* and *"saints,"* not dirty sinners saved by grace. We will discuss this fact in more detail later in the course. Did you notice the phrase, *"Grace to you and peace"* (v.7)? Paul uses this phrase in a majority of his epistles. Have you wondered why he did not say, peace and grace? Grace must be received before peace can be experienced. No doubt, the body of Christ should learn more about receiving God's grace.

Paul's Personal Message

No verse in the New Testament is more convicting than Romans 1:8. Paul states that the *"faith"* of the Roman believers was *"being proclaimed throughout the whole world."* As I first read this verse, I wondered if my faith is being proclaimed in my city, my county, or my state. One thing is certain: If my faith is not maturing and being enlarged, few will know that I am a follower of Christ. This is why I invest as much time as possible studying and praying through the Scriptures, for it is through our knowing and applying God's Word that our faith is broadened.

Verses 9-10 explain Paul's burden for these saints. He prayed for them *"unceasingly,"* asking that God allow him to visit Rome. He was genuinely concerned about their welfare, longing to see them firmly *"established"* in the faith (v.11). I don't view the *"spiritual gift"* mentioned in Romans 1:11 as one of the spiritual gifts of Romans 12:6-8, 1Corinthians 12 and 14, Ephesians 4, etc. I expect, rather, that Paul is referring to the spiritual growth that would occur in their lives as a result of his visit. On the heels of this thought, he makes an astounding statement. Paul, the mature man of God, declares that his time with the believers in Rome would serve to encourage him (Romans 1:12). Yes, a less mature believer can minister to the giants of the faith. We must never forget this truth!

Paul desired to bear *"fruit"* among the believers in Rome (v.13)—that is, allow Jesus to bear *"fruit"* through him. Even though he had experienced difficulty in arranging a visit, he refused to abandon the idea. In fact, in Romans 1:14-15 Paul mentions that he was *"...under obligation...to preach the gospel...,"* which should explain his desire to visit his readers. The words *"under obligation"* actually mean "in debt." Thus, Paul viewed himself as a debtor to the church at Rome. Can you believe Paul's heart? Can you believe the calling the Lord had placed upon him to preach to the Gentiles? Read 1Corinthians 9:16 for additional insight.

_____ *The Theme of the Epistle*

Verses 16-17 address Paul's view of *"the gospel."* First, he was *"...not ashamed of the gospel..."* (v.16). Why should he be ashamed of such good news? Today, many "water down" the gospel in the presence of those who might take offense. Paul was never guilty of this wrongdoing, for he understood that *"...the gospel...is the power of God for salvation to everyone who believes...."* Paul also realized that no other legitimate *"gospel"* existed (Galatians 1:8-10). The gospel of Christ was, and is, the only gospel with the power to transform lives.

> *The gospel of Christ was, and is, the only gospel with the power to transform lives.*

The reason the world is ashamed of the gospel is given in 1Corinthians 1:18:

> *For the word of the cross is to those who are perishing foolishness, but to us who are being saved it is the power of God.* (1Corinthians 1:18)

No doubt, *"...the word of the cross is to those who are perishing foolishness...."* The fact that God would die for the sin of the world is *"foolishness,"* or folly, to the lost—that is, so long as they reject Christ's perfect work. When they realize (in their depravity) that they are sinners in need of a Savior, however, the gospel becomes wonderful news. Don't ever forget this truth, especially when you endure scorn or ridicule from the lost. In fact, your greatest enemy today may become your most treasured comrade tomorrow. I am grateful for those who exemplified godly lives before me while I lived as an unbeliever. They were extremely offensive to me before I submitted to the Lord, but their willingness to risk the friendship for the sake of the truth spoke volumes concerning their courage and faith. I have since thanked them for loving me enough to demonstrate the more excellent way.

Notice, too, that Paul uses the phrase, *"...to the Jew first and also to the Greek"* (Romans 1:16). When Paul entered a city that he had not previously visited, he preferred preaching in the Jewish synagogue first, as is evidenced by the book of Acts. He believed that the gospel should be presented *"to the Jew first"* and then *"to the Greek"* (Gentiles). What had affected his thinking? The Law was given *"to the Jew first"* in Exodus 20. Also, our Lord instructed His disciples to preach *"to all the nations,"* beginning in *"Jerusalem,"* the city of the Jews (Luke 24:46-47).

Paul realized, too, that *"...the righteousness of God is revealed..."* in the gospel (Romans 1:17), for it is *"revealed"* through the cross of Christ. How so? God is holy. He will have nothing to do with sin, and must always judge sin. Man is unholy in his unredeemed state, inundated with sin—but capable of exercising personal repentance and faith while depraved. A just act took place on the cross since at that time sin was judged through the perfect God-man. Because *"righteousness"* means to be right, the Father's rightness was *"revealed"* when He judged sin through His sinless Son. Consequently, the gospel demonstrates *"the righteousness* [the rightness] *of God."*

The last phrase of Romans 1:17, which is taken from Habakkuk 2:4, could easily be the theme of this entire epistle:

> ...*But the righteous man shall live by faith.* (Romans 1:17)

This rock-solid truth basically sums up the book of Romans. Try to memorize this phrase. We will deal with it quite often in the weeks ahead, especially the terms *"righteous"* and *"faith."*

The Condemnation of the Heathen

Verses 18-32 explain the progression of sin in man. This section of Romans proves that a Godless society will self-destruct. We will now examine these verses more closely.

Paul first states that *"...the wrath of God is revealed...against all...who suppress the truth in unrighteousness"* (v.18). Every depraved (spiritually unregenerated) individual has opportunity to know and respond to God's *"truth."* Verses 19-20 state that even *"His eternal power and divine nature"* are revealed through what He has *"made"* in the physical realm. Why then do some not come to know God? The answer is given in Romans 1:18. They choose to *"suppress the truth"* through living *"in unrighteousness."* Yes, the unredeemed in most cases allow their morality to dictate their theology.

Be careful with verse 21. The phrase, *"For even though they knew God,"* does not mean that they *"knew"* Him in the sense of being part of His family, but that they only *"knew"* about Him How did they know about Him? They knew about Him through nature:

For since the creation of the world His invisible attributes, His eternal power and divine nature, have been clearly seen, being understood through what has been made, so that they are without excuse. (Romans 1:20)

We also find that *"they did not honor Him as God,"* causing their hearts to be *"darkened"* (v.21). The fruit of this darkened heart is mentioned in verses 22-23. They professed *"to be wise"* and *"became fools, and exchanged the glory of the incorruptible God for an image in the form of corruptible man and of birds and four-footed animals and crawling creatures."* No doubt, our previous statement continues to hold true: If a society chooses to reject God, that society will eventually self-destruct.

When man chose to reject truth (vv.18-23), *"God gave"* man *"over"* to something else (v.24). God is saying: "If you desire to discard truth and live in sin, I will release you to live in as much sin as you desire." Make sure to note the high price these individuals pay for their rebellion. In Romans 1:24-25, God *"gave them over"* to sexual *"impurity"* because *"they exchanged the truth...for a lie, and worshipped and served the creature rather than the Creator."* This is a picture of the downward spiral of mankind throughout history. First, truth is rejected; then comes sexual immorality, sex outside of marriage; and then man actually begins worshipping *"the creature rather than the Creator."* The sad part is that horrible consequences follow such sin. Considering the present condition of the world, it is obvious that infidelity rips a society to shreds.

The next stage is described in Romans 1:26-27:

For this reason God gave them over to degrading passions; for their women exchanged the natural function for that which is unnatural, and in the same way also the men abandoned the natural function of the woman and burned in their desire toward one another, men with men committing indecent acts and receiving in their own persons the due penalty of their error. (Romans 1:26-27)

"God gave them over to degrading passions" (homosexuality), for this stage is the next to last. When this occurs, time is normally short. (Realize that God loves the homosexual, but hates the homosexual's sin, just as He loves the adulterer, but hates the adulterer's sin.)

The final stage is a *"reprobate mind"* (Romans 1:28 KJV). This stage is described in verses 28-32, for mankind is no longer concerned with right and wrong. It is the final stage before a society is completely destroyed.

Where are we in America today? The answer is obvious. We are headed toward the last stage at an appalling rate. Can you see the need to equip ourselves with truth? A great battle awaits us, and we must be ready.

Romans 2 Questions

First Day

As you answer the following questions, ask the Lord to grant you wisdom.

1. Read Romans 2. In verses 1-16, Paul describes the moral man who does not know Christ. This man had been passing judgment on others (vv.1-3). Why will he be condemned? Who will condemn him? What does this convey regarding the importance of removing *"the log out of your own eye"* before judging others (Matthew 7:4-5)?

2. According to Romans 2:4, is it God's wrath or God's kindness that *"leads"* a person *"to repentance"?* (Repentance means to call sin by name and to turn from it.) How can knowing this truth assist you while sharing Christ with others?

Second Day

1. Read Romans 2. The man in verse 5 will receive the *"wrath"* of God due to the state of his *"heart."* What is said regarding the state of his *"heart"* (v.5)? What does this tell you about the importance of repentance?

2. According to Acts 11:18 and 2 Timothy 2:25, God grants repentance in the sense that He grants man the opportunity to repent while in his lost, depraved state. Is salvation possible without repentance? If not, why not?

3. Based on Romans 2:5, what are those without Christ *"storing up"?* How does this "storing up" tie in with Revelation 20:11-15? Does this judgment apply to believers and unbelievers, or does it apply to unbelievers alone?

4. How does the judgment mentioned in Romans 2:5 differ from the judgment addressed in 2Corinthians 5:10 and 1Corinthians 3:10-15? What encouragement do you draw from this?

Third Day

1.   Read Romans 2. How does Romans 2:6 relate to what we have addressed thus far? What is stated in Romans 2:7-10 about those who do *"evil"?* What do these same verses say about those who do *"good,"* that is, those who allow Jesus to do the *"good"* through them? Can you see how the contrast addressed in verses 7-10 confirms that God *"will render to every man according to his deeds"* (v.6). The next time the world tempts us to compromise, we must remember what Paul stresses here.

2.   From Romans 2:7-10, those who habitually do *"evil"* and enjoy it, proving that they have never repented and received Christ as Savior, will receive God's *"wrath."* Those who do *"good,"* if their *"good"* is performed through the dwelling Christ, will receive *"glory... honor and peace."* Write down any new thoughts below. Note: These verses do <u>not</u> teach, by any stretch of the imagination, that good deeds yield a right standing with God. Paul will confirm this truth later in the course, but for now quickly glance at Romans 3:20 and 3:28.

3.   Now that we have a basic understanding of verses 6-10, why would Paul follow by saying, *"For there is no partiality with God"* (v.11)?

Fourth Day

1.   Read Romans 2. According to verse 12, what will happen to individuals *"who have sinned without the Law,"* *"sinned"* meaning to live a lifestyle of habitual sin without accepting Christ as Savior? What will happen to those *"who have sinned under the Law,"* the word *"sinned"* possessing the same meaning as in the previous phrase? According to Romans 1:19-20, does everyone, even those who have not been exposed to the Law, have an opportunity to know about God? If so, through what avenue can they know that He exists? Is it possible to conclude, therefore, that God is just in judging those who have never heard the Law?

2.   What does verse 13 communicate to you? We must <u>not</u> view the phrase, *"but the doers of the Law will be justified,"* to mean that God justifies, or saves us, as a result of good works. Romans 3:20 and 3:28 verify that no one can become part of God's family through performing virtuous deeds. Jesus is the only doer of the Law, and for this reason salvation comes through Him alone. When we accept Christ, through exercising personal repentance and faith while depraved, God makes us not guilty before Him. In fact, He sees us as having lived the Law perfectly as a result of Jesus (who lived the Law perfectly) living in us (Galatians 2:20). How does this wonderful news encourage you?

3.   According to verses 14-15, do Gentiles who have not been exposed to *"the Law"* have an inward law *"written in their hearts"*? How could they have come to possess this inward law? In your opinion, were these Gentiles believers or unbelievers?

4.   The judgment mentioned in verse 16 is the *"great white throne"* judgment of Revelation 20:11-15. Who will do the judging? Who, then, will be sitting on the judgment throne of Revelation 20:11-15? Can those being judged conceal anything from their Judge (notice the word *"secrets"* in Romans 2:16)?

Fifth Day

1.   Read Romans 2. Verses 17-29 explain why being a *"Jew,"* or trusting in *"the Law,"* or *"circumcision,"* <u>cannot</u> make a person right with God. Why would an unsaved Jew in Paul's day, or even in our day, have a problem with this teaching?

2.   From Romans 2:17-24, James 2:10, and Romans 3:28, why are Jews unable to obtain a right standing with God so long as they trust in the Law for salvation? What do verses 23 and 24 communicate regarding the witness of a person living under Law? Do you detect a lack of joy in their lives? According to 2Corinthians 3:6, why does this exist?

3.   According to Romans 2:25, under what condition can *"circumcision"* make a person right with God? Has anyone lived up to this standard outside of Jesus?

4.   Verses 26-27 are extremely interesting. Paul contrasts the unbelieving Jew who is circumcised with the uncircumcised Gentile who is a believer. When we accept Jesus as Savior in our depraved state, God makes us new and justifies us, that is, makes us not guilty before Him. From then on He sees us as having kept the Law perfectly. He also sends the Holy Spirit to direct our lives, which allows our behavior to begin to line up with the righteous standard of the Law (Romans 8:4)—a topic addressed in much depth in the weeks ahead. With this in mind, record what verses 26-27 communicate to you.

Sixth Day

1.   Read Romans 2. Who is a true *"Jew"* (Romans 2:28-29)? Does this mean that God is no longer concerned with fulfilling the unconditional covenants He made with the physical Jewish nation? Think long and hard before answering.

2.   Would you rather be praised by man or by God (v.29)? What encouraged you the most from Romans 2? Record your thoughts and read the following lesson. Hopefully, the lesson will shed new light on some of your unanswered questions.

Romans 2 Lesson

Romans 2 can be divided into two sections. The first section condemns the moral man who does not know Christ (vv.1-16), while the second condemns the Jew who does not know Christ (vv.17-29). As you study this lesson, realize that Romans 2:1-16 is one of the most challenging sections of the course. Digest what you can, therefore, and leave the remainder for later.

The Condemnation of the Moral Man

Had we lived in Paul's day, we would have heard the moral man say, "Preach on, Paul! You are exactly right! The man who sins to the degree that you have discussed in Romans 1:18-32 is deserving of judgment! Tell it like it is, Paul!"

Paul had a word for the good, upstanding, self-righteous, moral man, who trusted in his good works: *"You are without excuse,"* Paul told him. Why was this man without excuse? He was practicing *"the same things"* (v.1)! He may not have been practicing them outwardly, but he was practicing them within his heart. The man in Romans 2:1-16 didn't know the Lord any more intimately than the man in Romans 1:18-32, for neither had repented and exercised faith in Christ. After all, repentance means to call sin what it is and to turn from it.

Have you attempted to share Jesus with a good upstanding citizen, a dedicated church worker, a faithful father who provides for his family, or any such outwardly pure individual who has failed to accept Christ as Savior? Of all the people that Paul mentions, this type may be the most deceived. In most cases, it is easier to address the man described in Romans 1:18-32. One thing is certain: No difference exists. Both will be condemned to eternal punishment unless they choose to repent and exercise faith while depraved. Romans 2:2-3 states this truth very plainly.

Romans 2:4 is one of the most powerful verses in the entire New Testament.

> *Or do you think lightly of the riches of His kindness and forbearance and patience, not knowing that the kindness of God leads you to repentance?*
> (Romans 2:4)

For years, I believed that a knowledge of God's wrath is the main player in bringing the lost to repentance. I then read this passage, and something clicked. It is not God's wrath but His *"kindness"* that motivates the depraved to turn from sin! Do you comprehend the significance of this statement? Christ's death on the cross and the love that our Father displayed there, along with His daily *"kindness,"* reveal to unregenerate man that *"God is love"* (1John 4:8, 16). This truth serves as a tremendous catalyst for the depraved to repent and exercise faith in Christ. Truly, the greatest motivator is God's love—never His wrath! Note: The Law convicts the lost (depraved) of their need for a Savior as well. This will be addressed shortly.

> *It is not God's wrath but His "kindness" that motivates the depraved to turn from sin!*

No doubt, God requires repentance from those who desire to be saved. Thus, God grants the depraved the right and freedom to repent (Acts 11:18; 2Timothy 2:25), for *"repentance...leads to life"* as well as *"to the knowledge of the truth":*

> *...Well then, God has granted to the Gentiles also the repentance that leads to life.* (Acts 11:18)

> *...if perhaps God may grant them repentance leading to the knowledge of the truth,* (2Timothy 2:25)

Note: These two verses are covered in greater depth in Week 7 of the course.

Until a person comes to Christ through personal repentance and faith, the deeper truths of God are unattainable. Of course, the depraved possess ample truth to repent and believe. Nature continually reveals the Godhead to the lost as well as the saved (Romans 1:20).

Repentance also applies once we are saved. Knowing *"the kindness of God"* (Romans 2:4), we confess and repent soon after sins are committed. We will discuss this subject in more detail as we progress.

Romans 2:5 states that even the moral man will receive God's *"wrath"* due to his *"stubbornness and unrepentant heart."* Paul also states that the lost are *"storing up wrath for...the day of wrath"* (v.5). Do you realize that God's *"wrath"* will be poured out on unbelievers in proportion to the amount of *"wrath"* they have stored up—in proportion to the degree of their sin? They will face the *"great white throne"* judgment (Revelation 20:11-15), a judgment of condemnation for all who have refused to exercise repentance and faith while depraved. This *"judgment"* will be *"righteous"* (Romans 2:5), which means that it will be just and upright. The unrepentant man will receive exactly what he deserves. After all, he had every opportunity to believe.

The *"great white throne"* judgment (Revelation 20:11) differs from *"the judgment seat of Christ"* (2Corinthians 5:10). No believer will be judged at the *"great white throne,"* for it is a judgment of wrath. A New Testament believer faces *"the judgment seat of Christ,"* a judgment of rewards. Each of our works will be tested *"with fire"* (1Corinthians 3:10-15), and we will be rewarded for deeds done in faith.

> *N*o believer will be judged at the *"great white throne,"* for it is a judgment of wrath.

God *"...will render to every man according to his deeds"* (Romans 2:6) Those who do *"good"* will receive *"glory...honor...peace... and immortality, eternal life"* (vv.7, 10). Those who *"do not obey the truth"* receive *"wrath...indignation...tribulation and distress"* (vv.8-9). According to verses 7-10, all who habitually do *"evil"* and enjoy it, proving that they have never repented of sin and accepted Christ as Savior, will receive God's *"wrath."* All who do *"good,"* if their good deeds result from yielding to Christ's indwelling presence, will receive *"glory...honor and peace."* After studying this comparison, do you wonder how anyone could choose to reject Christ? Note: These verses do *not* teach that good deeds yield a right standing with God. Paul will confirm this fact to a greater degree in subsequent verses.

Verse 11 confirms that *"...there is no partiality with God."* Any person who is unsaved, due to refusing to repent and believe while depraved, will be condemned and *"thrown into the lake of fire"* (Revelation 20:15). Yes, God loves man enough to allow man to live eternally separated from His presence should he (man) so desire.

Paul makes an extremely interesting statement in Romans 2:12.

> *For all who have sinned without the Law will also perish without the Law; and*
> *all who have sinned under the Law will be judged by the Law;* (Romans 2:12)

Paul teaches that *"all who have sinned without the Law will also perish without the Law."* *"Sinned"* in this instance points to a lifestyle of habitual sin without receiving Christ as Savior. Is it fair for God to respond to the unsaved in this manner? Can individuals who have never been exposed to the Law, the Law given to Moses, know about God? They certainly can, for we learned in Romans 1:20 that God's creation reveals *"...His invisible attributes, His eternal power and divine nature..."* We realize, too, that many exercised repentance and faith and were declared righteous by God before Moses received the Law. Therefore, Paul's statement in verse 12 is a fair one.

In addition, we know that *"all who have sinned under the Law will be judged by the Law"* (v.12). *"Sinned"* again points to a lifestyle of habitual sin without receiving Christ as Savior. Thus, everyone who has been exposed to the Law, and has refused to accept Christ while depraved, *"will be judged by the Law"* at the great white throne judgment. In other words, those who have heard the Law but have refused to believe in the *"seed"* of Genesis 3:15, who *"is Christ"* (Galatians 3:16), have not received a *"just"* standing *"before God"* (v.13).

> *for not the hearers of the Law are just before God, but the doers of the Law will be justified.* (Romans 2:13)

Paul's last statement in verse 13, when studied in context, brings much into focus:

> *...but the doers of the Law will be justified.* (Romans 2:13)

How can individuals be *"doers of the Law"* (v.13) if when they break the Law on one count they are guilty of breaking it on all counts (James 2:10)? We can be *"doers of the Law"* under one condition only—if we repent and exercise faith in Christ, Who lived the Law perfectly (Galatians 4:4; Hebrews 4:15) and takes up residence in us <u>after</u> we repent and believe while depraved (Galatians 2:20). Through Jesus living in us (Galatians 2:20) and our living in Jesus (2Corinthians 5:17; Ephesians 2:6) God justifies us by taking away our guilt and seeing us as having lived the Law perfectly. Thus, it is Jesus' life in us, the God-man Who <u>did</u> the Law perfectly, that allows the Father to view us as *"doers of the Law."* We will deal with justification in more detail in Romans 5.

> *God justifies us by taking away our guilt and seeing us as having lived the Law perfectly.*

The statements, *"do instinctively the things of the Law"* (v.14) and *"they show the work of the Law written in their hearts"* (v.15), are challenging to interpret. If they point to the work of the Holy Spirit in a New Testament believer, these Gentiles are believers. If they address the moral law written on the conscience of every man, these Gentiles are unbelievers. Several scholars agree with the second scenario because of verse 16, which speaks of the judgment of the ungodly at the *"great white throne"* (Revelation 20:11). No believer will face this judgment, yet the individuals of verses 14-15 seem to be present when this judgment occurs. If the second scenario is correct, these Gentiles are lost and without eternal life. One fact is certain: *"The secrets of"* the lost will be judged (Romans 2:16, Revelation 20:11-15). No sin or motive will be veiled, not even among the morally pure who have rejected Christ's provision. All sin will be exposed.

The Condemnation of the Jew

The second half of this chapter, consisting of verses 17-29, explains why the unbelieving Jew will be condemned. Up to verse 17 the Jews could say, "Preach on, Paul, we are in total agreement." Paul had not yet discussed, in depth at least, what occurs when a Jew rejects Christ.

The Hebrew male normally viewed himself as right with God based on three counts: (1) He was a Jew (2) He had been circumcised (3) The Jews had received the Law and were, therefore, God's chosen people. All or any of these provided a ticket to heaven as far as the average Jew was concerned. Paul disagrees. He spends the remainder of the chapter, along with part of the next, explaining why.

The Jews who rejected Jesus' Messiahship assumed that their Jewishness made them part of God's family (v.17). Paul refutes their argument in verses 28-29 by stating that a *"Jew"* is not a true *"Jew"* until the *"Spirit"* has circumcised his *"heart."* This circumcision occurs in conjunction with the New Testament believer being placed *"in Christ"* (2Corinthians 5:17) subsequent to exercising repentance and faith while depraved (Acts 16:31; Romans 10:9-10). By no stretch of the imagination is Paul teaching that the church has replaced physical Israel as God's chosen people, as some have incorrectly assumed. We will address this topic in more detail shortly.

In verses 17-24, Paul mentions the disparity between possessing the Law and living by its requirements. He writes, in fact, that those *"who boast"* about possessing *"the Law...dishonor God" "through...breaking"* the Law's commands (v.23)!

Paul discusses *"circumcision"* in verses 25-29, for the unbelieving Jews perceived physical circumcision as securing a right standing before God. This arrangement could not be the case, for Abraham was circumcised <u>after</u> he was declared righteous (read Genesis 15:6 and Genesis 17:24). Actually, circumcision was given to the Jewish nation as *"...a seal of the righteousness of the faith which he* [Abraham] *had while uncircumcised..."* (Romans 4:11). In other words, circumcision was a reminder to the Jewish nation that faith, exercised in one's lost and spiritually unregenerated state, results in God granting salvation.

In verses 26-29, Paul contrasts a New Testament believer with the Jew who is trusting in *"circumcision"* for salvation by stressing the difference between *"outward"* and inward *"circumcision."* The *"heart"* of a church saint is circumcised by *"the Spirit"* (Romans 2:29). Once we are empowered by the *"Spirit,"* our behavior will begin to line up with the righteous standard of the Law, a subject covered in greater depth in Romans 8:4. A man who is trusting in physical circumcision, however, must keep the whole Law without breaking a single command— and he must do so by means of his own power and strength. Such a scenario is a total impossibility (Romans 3:20, 28).

Understanding verses 28-29 is essential. Do you realize that when depraved Jews or Gentiles exercise repentance and faith during the church age they become members of the body of Christ, the universal church? This does not mean, however, that the church is fulfilling God's unconditional covenants granted to the physical Jewish nation. For example, God promised Abram that he and his physical descendants, the physical Jewish nation, would possess the territory *"...From the river of Egypt as far as the great river, the river Euphrates"* (Genesis 13:15; 15:18; 17:8). The Jews will not possess this land until the Millennium, the one-thousand year reign of Christ on the earth (Revelation 20:4, 6). This total possession of the land (all of it, not just some of it) must occur if God is to remain faithful to His Word.

Many have misunderstood Romans 2:28-29 and accepted the following error: Because a true Jew is one who is circumcised inwardly, and since every member of the body of Christ fits this category, God is not obligated to fulfill the unconditional covenants granted to the <u>physical</u> Jewish nation. In fact, God is done with the physical Jewish nation and is concerned with the church alone.

How can this be if God is faithful to His Word? He promised a literal nation a literal land, along with other unconditional promises as well. He must fulfill these promises if He is the God of truth and faithfulness. We will address this in more detail later in the study.

*M*ake sure to desire the *"praise...from God"* rather than the *"praise...from men."*

Enjoy your day off tomorrow. As you do so, make sure to desire the *"praise...from God"* rather than the *"praise...from men"* (v.29).

Romans 3:1-8 Questions

First Day

Today's lesson may be challenging, but remember: We are laying a foundation that will support the truths of Romans 5-8. Foundations must be strong, but they are not easily constructed.

After Paul's words of Romans 2:17-29, the unbelieving Jews asked a series of questions in an attempt to undermine Paul's theology. These questions are recorded in verses 1, 3, 5, 7 and 8 of Romans 3, while Paul's answers are documented in verses 2, 4, 6, and 8 of the same chapter. Therefore, verses 1-8 record the standard argument presented by an unbelieving Jew after hearing Paul's teaching. These verses also include Paul's responses. Ask the Lord for ample wisdom to understand what is presented here.

1. Read Romans 3:1-8. Two questions are asked in verse 1: _"Then what advantage has the Jew?"_ and _"Or what is the benefit of circumcision?"_ How would you answer these questions?

2. Why would a Jew ask the previous two questions? To answer correctly, put yourself in the place of those Jews who had heard Paul's teaching but had trusted in their Jewish heritage, the Law, and circumcision for salvation.

Second Day

1. Read Romans 3:1-8. From Romans 3:2, how did Paul answer the questions of Romans 3:1?

2. What are the _"oracles of God"?_ What is stated about them in Acts 7:37-38?

3. Read Exodus 34:27-35 along with 2Corinthians 3:1-18, and contrast the old and new covenants.

4. How does Paul describe the old covenant in 2Corinthians 3:6-9? How does this tie in with Exodus 20:18-21 and Hebrews 12:18-24.

5.   According to Galatians 3:24, what is the purpose of the *"Law,"* the old covenant? Write down any new thoughts the Lord gave you as you researched today's questions.

Third Day

1.   Read Romans 3:1-8. Verse 3 asks an extremely interesting question. Will God's *"faithfulness,"* His *"faithfulness"* to the Jews who repent and believe while depraved, be nullified if a great number of the Jews prove to be unfaithful by rejecting Christ? Why would the unbelieving Jew ask such a question?

2.   Write down at least one instance in the Old Testament where God was faithful to the believing remnant of the Jews when the majority of the nation remained in unbelief. Many such instances exist, so take your pick.

3.   Do you picture God as a faithful God? Read 2Timothy 1:12, 1Corinthians 10:13, 1Corinthians 1:9, 1Thessalonians 5:24, 2Thessalonians 3:3, Hebrews 2:17, Hebrews 3:6, Hebrews 10:23, Hebrews 11:11, 1Peter 4:19, 1John 1:9, Revelation 1:5, Revelation 19:11, and Revelation 21:5 to grasp what New Testament Scripture declares regarding His faithfulness. How do these verses encourage you?

4.   Many verses in God's Word describe God's faithfulness. Which verse encourages you most?

Fourth Day

1.   Read Romans 3:1-8. Based on Romans 3:4, what was Paul's opinion of God's faithfulness?

2.   In Romans 3:4, Paul writes, *"...let God be found true, though every man be found a liar...."* What does this statement communicate to you? Would you continue to view God as being *"true"* and worthy of serving if everyone you know should deny Him?

3. The last two phrases of Romans 3:4 say, *"...That Thou mightest be justified in Thy words, and mightest prevail when Thou art judged."* The phrase *"Thou art judged"* can be interpreted *"dost enter into judgment."* When God passes judgment, why can no one rightly accuse Him of being unfair or unjust in doing so?

Fifth Day

1. Read Romans 3:1-8. Is it possible, in any circumstance, for *"our unrighteousness"* to demonstrate *"the righteousness of God"* (v.5)? Why would the unbelieving Jew ask such a senseless question?

2. If the sin of man should demonstrate God's righteousness, in other words bring glory to Him, could God judge the lost and remain just? If not, why not?

3. In Romans 3:6, Paul answers the question of Romans 3:5. We understand from verse 6 that God will *"judge the world."* What judgment is Paul indicating if *"the world"* points to the unsaved? (For help, review the third question from Week 2, second day?) You are almost finished with this week's questions. Things will start to ease up next week. I Promise!

Sixth Day

1. Read Romans 3:1-8. Verses 7 and 8 are fascinating, for they present the final attempt of the unbelieving Jews to undermine Paul's theology. They reveal the mentality that sometimes results when Law is elevated above God's grace. Describe this mindset? Does this not amplify your desire to abandon Law and bask in God's grace?

2. You have completed the portion of Romans that verifies why a Jew who rejects Christ is condemned (Romans 2:17-3:8). What has been the most exciting truth you have learned from this section? How will this input benefit you while sharing Christ with an unbelieving Jew?

Romans 3:1-8 Lesson

Attacks from Paul's Jewish Opponents

Life is extremely hard for those who cling to the Law (the Law given to Israel through Moses). Are you prepared to explore the mentality of those who choose Law over grace? Romans 3:1-8 reveals some of the arguments that the unbelieving Jews hurled at Paul as he carried the gospel to the world.

As you study these eight verses, you should link them to Romans 2:17-29 which is part of the complete section of Romans 2:17-3:8 that deals entirely with the Jews. We must remember that the unbelieving Jewish male considered himself right with God on three counts: (1) He was a descendent of Abraham, and thereby a Jew (2) He was part of the nation that had received the Law (3) He had been circumcised. As far as he was concerned, any or all of the above would do the job. But Paul's gospel stated that man, any man, be he Jew or Gentile, was right with God only if he had, while depraved, repented and chosen to receive Christ as Savior. We can only imagine the degree to which the unbelieving Jews resented Paul's teaching.

To properly understand verses 1-8, we must consider the circumstances under which they were written. According to Paul's theology, the Jews could no longer view their Jewishness, the Law, or circumcision as providing a righteous standing before God. Paul had annihilated all of these arguments in Romans 2:17-29. Consequently, their only alternative was to attack Paul's theology. Paul, therefore, addresses the questions he must have faced time after time as he shared the gospel with the unbelieving Jews.

Romans 3:1 records two of these questions: *"Then what advantage has the Jew?" "Or what is the benefit of circumcision?"* No doubt, Paul's Jewish opponents were bewildered to the point of asking: "If what you are teaching is true, does being a Jew carry any advantage at all?!" Paul is quick to answer, stating that there is *"Great"* advantage to being Jewish and much benefit in circumcision (Romans 3:2). After all, the Jews have been *"entrusted with the oracles of God"!*

The *"oracles of God,"* also mentioned in Acts 7:37-38, were received by Moses on Mount Sinai. Hence, the word *"oracles"* in this case is synonymous with the Law. As we learned from Romans 1:20, God initially revealed Himself to mankind through creation. That revelation was minor, however, compared to the degree to which He revealed Himself through the Law, for an oracle is a divine communication or revelation. Through these *"oracles,"* the Jewish nation had an opportunity to know God in a way that had not been provided to the Gentiles. No other nation had received such a revelation. Thus, the advantage afforded the Jewish nation was unmistakable.

The Father requires repentance and faith from the depraved (the lost) prior to delivering them from the Law and awarding them new "life" in Christ.

The unbelieving Jews, however, misinterpreted the Law's purpose. Instead of allowing it to reveal their sin and confirm their need for the Savior, they perceived it as an end in itself. In fact, the Law (Genesis through Deuteronomy) and the Prophets (Isaiah through Malachi) were passionately memorized, but had little impact on their daily living due to their disobedience. Their devotion to the law but lack of application is vividly portrayed in Matthew 2:3-6, for the Jewish leaders revealed to Herod the exact location of the Messiah's birth yet were directly responsible for His death (Matthew 27:20). No doubt, they knew the letter of the Law but did not know the God who gave the letter.

The Father requires repentance and faith from the depraved (the lost) prior to delivering them from the Law and awarding them new *"life"* in Christ (read 2Corinthians 3:1-18). Note 2Corinthians 3:16:

"but whenever a man turns to the Lord, the veil is taken away." (2Corinthians 3:16)

The combination of Exodus 34:27-35 and 2Corinthians 3:1-18 reveals that the old covenant (Law) is temporary while the *"new covenant"* is eternal. Paul's intriguing comparison in 2Corinthians 3:6-9 of the old covenant with the new states that *"the letter* [the old covenant] *kills, but the Spirit* [the new covenant] *gives life"* (v.6). He also speaks of *"the ministry of death"* (v.7) and *"condemnation"* (v.9) brought on by the Law. Exodus 20:18-21 and Hebrews 12:18-24 prove as well that the Law cannot bring a person into a place of intimacy with the Creator. The Law was given as a *"tutor to lead us to Christ"* (Galatians 3:24; 1Timothy 1:8-11) so the depraved might repent and believe.

Have you noticed that when a system of thought is discredited, the members of that system often misrepresent the views of those who have proven them incorrect? The unsaved Jews used the same approach with Paul's theology. As you will see, their arguments did nothing to sway Paul or disprove the truth of his gospel.

Romans 3:3 contains a question directed to Paul by his Jewish opponents.

> *...If some did not believe, their unbelief will not nullify the faithfulness of God, will it?* (Romans 3:3)

These Jews were asking: "Suppose that Christ is the Messiah mentioned in the Law and the Prophets but some of us do not believe. Will not God be obligated to save the whole Jewish nation?" Their goal was to prove that if God should save a portion of the Jewish nation He would be obligated to save the whole nation. They believed the converse as well, that if God should condemn a portion of the nation He would be required to condemn the whole nation. These men failed to realize that God is faithful to His promises relating to salvation, regardless of the number of people who accept Christ as Savior. God is faithful! He has been faithful since creation and will continue to be faithful throughout eternity. If all of your friends reject the gospel, deny Christ, curse Him, walk away and never look back, His faithfulness to you will remain steadfast.

An example of God's faithfulness is seen in 2Kings 22-23. Almost all of the Kingdom of Judah had submitted to sin, and the Law of God was no longer perceived as the standard for righteous living. Then Josiah, a godly king, reinstated the Law. God, however, needed no reinstating. He had remained faithful to the believing remnant even while the majority of the nation floundered in sin. Time and time again, God has displayed His relentless faithfulness, and the wonderful news is that it continues today! Consequently, when *"...we are faithless, He remains faithful..."* (2Timothy 2:13). Wasn't it encouraging to read about His faithfulness in 2Timothy 1:12, 1Corinthians 10:13, 1Corinthians 1:9, 1Thessalonians 5:24, 2Thessalonians 3:3, Hebrews 2:17, Hebrews 3:6, and other similar passages as you answered this week's questions?

In Romans 3:4, Paul responds to the unbelieving Jews' question of Romans 3:3 using the strongest language possible, *"May it never be!"* *"May it never be"* that the overall unbelief within the Jewish nation should nullify God's faithfulness to the Jews who believe. Paul understood well that God will *"be found true, though every man be found a liar."* Not stopping here, he goes on to say, *"That Thou mightest be justified in Thy words, and mightest prevail when Thou art judged."* The words, *"art judged,"* can be interpreted, *"dost enter into judgment."* Therefore, the last phrase of the passage can be rendered: *"and mightest prevail when Thou dost enter into judgment."* Yes, when God passes judgment, no one, not even an unbelieving Jew, can accuse Him of being unfair or unjust.

The Law was given as a "tutor to lead us to Christ."

Paul addresses *"unrighteousness"* and how it relates to God's *"righteousness"* in verse 5. Evidently, the Jews who disagreed with Paul's gospel had said: "What you are teaching proves that *'our unrighteousness demonstrates the righteousness of God.'* In fact, if our acts of disobedience present opportunity for God's righteousness to be manifested to an ever increasing degree, which in turn enhances His reputation, how can He condemn our sin? In fact, we need to sin to a greater degree so His righteousness can be manifested all the more." Can you believe that they would make such outlandish statements?

Consider the dilemma facing mankind should this absurdity be true. First, not one person would be judged and God would not be God; He would have no right to sit on the throne of the universe. Second, if God did not judge sin, the world would be locked in sin for all eternity. Third, if man's sin enhanced God's reputation and He judged such sin, He would be totally unjust!

From the arguments the Jews presented, it is obvious that man dislikes admitting his wrong. To grow in the knowledge of the Lord, however, we must remain teachable, never hardened by sin's deceitfulness, always maintaining a willingness to admit our error.

To grow in the knowledge of the Lord we must remain teachable, never hardened by sin's deceitfulness, always maintaining a willingness to admit our error.

To understand Romans 3:6, we must realize that the unsaved Jew perceived God's judgment as directed toward Gentiles only. Paul points out, however, that it would be impossible for God to *"judge the world"* should He fail to judge the unbelieving Jew. The judgment addressed here is the *"great white throne"* judgment of Revelation 20:11-15, a judgment directed toward those who reject God's provision through Christ.

In Romans 3:7-8, Paul's enemies make their final assault. They accuse him of teaching, *"Let us do evil that good may come."* In effect, they were accusing Paul of granting man a license to sin. Bondage to the Law many times produces such erroneous thinking.

Are you realizing what Law does? It kills and defeats and destroys, and that is its purpose. However, remaining under Law eventually leads to license, which advocates that man is free to sin as much as he likes. Those who adhere to this lie eventually say, *"Let us do evil that good may come."* If good sprang from evil, however, evil would be the source of good, making absolute truth nonexistent. Thus, Paul refutes every argument generated by the unbelieving Jews.

Our study of Romans 3:1-8 may be summed up in one statement: "The strictest legalism leads to the greatest license" (source unknown). May we forever be delivered from the bondage of the Law through the grace we have been granted in Christ!

Our foundation is getting stronger. In fact, three more weeks of study and it will easily support the amazing truths of Romans 5-8.

Romans 3:9-31 Questions

First Day

1. Read Romans 3:9-31. Don't forget to pray for wisdom. List the different classes of people that Paul condemned in Romans 1:18-32, Romans 2:1-16, and Romans 2:17-3:8.

2. Paul condemns the whole world, that is, the lost world in Romans 3:9-18. In your opinion, why would he do so at this stage of this epistle? Hint: Consider whom he has condemned previously. Also, consider what he states in verse 9.

3. Within the parameters of verses 10-18, Paul also describes the characteristics of a society that does not know God. Which of these characteristics are most prevalent today? Which ones concern you most, and why?

Second Day

1. Read Romans 3:9-31. Paul explains the purpose of the Law in Romans 3:19-20. What is that purpose?

2. In your own words, what does it mean to *"become accountable to God"* (v.19)?

3. Through the avenue of Law, can man work his way into a right standing with God? If not, why not (v.20)?

4. Have you attempted to live the Christian life under Law? If so, what occurred? Would you classify your attempt as successful? Think about verses 19 and 20 over the next few days. You might even memorize them.

Third Day

1. Read Romans 3:21-31. According to Romans 3:21, *"...apart from the Law the righteousness of God has been manifested..."* What does this mean? What does this communicate regarding the Person of Christ?

2.   With reference to this same verse (v.21), do *"the Law and the Prophets,"* the Old Testament Scriptures in other words, actually witness (speak) of God imparting His *"righteousness" "apart from the Law"?* If so, list some examples of where this occurs.

3.   According to Romans 3:22, God imparts *"righteousness"* to whom? How does 2Corinthians 5:21 relate to this passage?

Fourth Day

1.   Read Romans 3:21-31. Taking into consideration Paul's words of Romans 1:18-3:18, why would he now say, *"...for all have sinned and fall short of the glory of God"* (v.23)? What does Paul mean when he says, *"all have sinned"?*

2.   Why would Paul want his readers to understand that *"all"* who do not know Christ *"fall short of the glory of God"* (v.23)? Why does lost mankind *"fall short"* of this *"glory"?* If you had difficulty answering this question, the next few questions, and answers, should tie everything together.

3.   According to John 1:14 and Colossians 1:27, through what avenue does a New Testament believer receive this *"glory"?* How does this increase your appreciation for what Christ accomplished through His death, burial, and resurrection?

4.   God's *"glory,"* which Christ personifies in the New Testament, is seen throughout the Old Testament in the form of a cloud or fire. Read the following verses and record any new insights: Exodus 3:2; 13:21-22; 19:16-18; 40:34; 2Chronicles 5:13-14; Ezekiel 11:22-25; Luke 2:8-9; John 1:14; Acts 1:9, 2:3; Colossians 1:27.

Fifth Day

1.   Read Romans 3:21-31. Paul uses three more than significant terms in verse 24: *"justified," "grace,"* and *"redemption."* Define these terms in your own words. To do so, you may need assistance from outside sources.

2. Now that you have defined *"justified," "grace,"* and *"redemption,"* write out what Romans 3:24 communicates to you.

3. In Romans 3:25, you see the term *"propitiation"* (New American Standard). What does it mean? How does it tie in with Hebrews 9:5, realizing that the same Greek word used for *"propitiation"* in Romans 3:25 is interpreted *"mercy seat"* in Hebrews 9:5? If you have difficulty answering today's questions, help is on the way in this week's lesson. Remember, however, to exhaust all resources before reading the portion of the lesson that relates to your unanswered questions.

4. Verse 25 states, *"This was to demonstrate His righteousness."* How does the cross of Christ *"demonstrate"* God's *"righteousness"?*

5. Romans 3:25 also contains the phrase, *"He passed over the sins previously committed."* Paul is referring to sins committed by believers who lived prior to the cross. What is Paul saying here, and how does it relate to Hebrews 9:11-12, Hebrews 10:4, 10:11, and 10:14? Make sure to digest what you are learning about the superiority of the blood of Christ.

Sixth Day

1. Read Romans 3:21-31. What does Paul say about *"faith"* in verses 27-30? According to verse 27, can those who exercise faith while depraved boast before God? If not, why not?

2. To whom is Paul referring when he speaks of *"the circumcised"* and *"the uncircumcised"* (v.30)? Ephesians 2:11-12 will assist you in answering this question.

3. How is it that *"we establish the Law...through faith"* (v.31)?

Romans 3:9-31 Lesson

The Condemnation of the Whole World

Paul has condemned the heathen (Romans 1:18-32), the moral man (Romans 2:1-16), and the Jew (Romans 2:17-3:8). Now he condemns the whole world (Romans 3:9-18). He has already proven *"...that both Jews and Greeks are all under sin"* (verse 9). In verses 10-18, however, he describes the condition of a society that does not know Christ. Paul's words should make all of us sit up and take notice. I cannot help but compare his description of the world with the world we live in today. When man refuses to fear God, destruction is inevitable—no matter what stage of history.

Righteousness by Faith, not through the Law

Good news is forthcoming in Romans 3:19! God, in His mercy, spoke *"the Law"* into existence to shut man's *"mouth"* and make him *"accountable to God."* Simply put, the Law was given to reveal man's sin and show him his need for a Savior. It was given, in other words, to bring man to repentance (vv.19-20), *"...for through the Law comes the knowledge of sin."* That was the Law's function then, and it remains the same today. The Law was given so man would cease trying to please God by his own efforts and submit to His saving grace. Paul's statement in verse 20 is so very true!

> *...by the works of the Law no flesh will be justified in His sight; for through the Law comes the knowledge of sin.* (Romans 3:20)

According to verse 21, even better news is on the horizon!

> *But now apart from the Law the righteousness of God has been manifested, being witnessed by the Law and the Prophets.* (Romans 3:21)

The word *"righteousness"* means "to be made right with God—to be free of guilt, or to be justified." Paul's point is that a right standing with God can be attained *"apart from the Law,"* and that such is *"witnessed by"* the portion of the Bible known as *"the Law and the Prophets."* For example, Abraham came on the scene in Genesis, a portion of the Bible known as *"the Law,"* consisting of Genesis through Deuteronomy. In fact, Abraham is first mentioned in Genesis 11:26-32. In Genesis 15:6, however, he is declared righteous on the basis of faith, prior to God issuing the Law in Exodus 20. This order of events proves that God can declare a man righteous *"apart from the Law"* given to Israel. Clearly, this *"righteousness,"* which God grants *"apart from the Law,"* is described in Genesis, one of the five books of the Bible titled *"the Law."* Thus, Romans 3:21 makes a more than valid statement.

A right standing with God can be attained "apart from the Law."

This *"righteousness"* is also *"witnessed by...the Prophets."* For instance, Isaiah the prophet, in Isaiah 53, *"witnessed"* (prophesied) that a suffering Savior, Jesus, would die for the sin of man and be the avenue through which *"righteousness"* is bestowed upon believers. Romans 4:6-8 also teaches that David, a prophet, spoke *"of the blessings upon the man to whom God reckons righteousness apart from works,"* that is, *"apart from"* the *"works"* of the Law. Again we see more support for Romans 3:21.

In verse 22, Paul confirms that God imparts *"righteousness"* on the basis of *"faith in Jesus Christ."* Yes, God made us as righteous as He is righteous through placing us *"in Christ"*

(2Corinthians 5:17, 21) subsequent to our repenting and believing while depraved. This gift of *"righteousness"* is why we are saints instead of lowly sinners saved by grace!!

Romans 3:23 has more depth than the reader can fathom at first glance. It declares:

> *for all have sinned and fall short of the glory of God*, (Romans 3:23)

Paul has made it very clear that *"all have sinned."* To comprehend the significance of the second phrase, *"and fall short of the glory of God,"* we must dig deeper.

The phrase, *"the glory of God,"* points to the physical manifestation of God's presence—which appeared in the Old Testament in the form of a cloud and (or) fire. This glory appeared to Moses in Exodus 3:2 and to Israel in Exodus 13:21-22 and Exodus 19:16-18. It reappeared and remained on the earth after the completion of the tabernacle in Exodus 40:34-38, even filling King Solomon's temple in 2Chronicles 5:13-14. This same glory departed from Jerusalem and ascended into heaven in Ezekiel 11:22-25, remaining there until Luke 2:8-9. Because Jesus is the *"glory"* of God (John 1:14), the glory returned to earth in the Person of Christ. After Jesus' resurrection, the glory ascended into heaven (Acts 1:9), only to reappear on the day of Pentecost (Acts 2:3) to live in every New Testament believer. Consequently, God placed His *"glory"* inside us (Colossians 1:27) subsequent to our exercising repentance and faith while depraved (Acts 16:31; Romans 10:9-10). What wonderful news!

"Justified" in Romans 3:24 means *"to be made righteous (right) in the eyes of God."* Thus, if you are a believer, the Father views you as having never sinned. He also sees you as never sinning again. Consider too that we were *"justified as a gift by His grace," "grace"* being defined as "unmerited favor." God's justification of the New Testament believer is, therefore, a *"gift."* It most definitely is not earned. After all, *"faith,"* exercised while depraved, is anything but a *"work"* (Romans 3:27; 4:5; 9:32).

Even more good news is forthcoming. *"Redemption"* (v.24) means "to be set free, to liberate by paying a price." Therefore, our sins were redeemed (paid for) on the cross by God's grace. In addition, our sinful nature was eradicated through Christ's death, which will be addressed in Romans 6. Thus, we were *"justified"* (made righteous) by God's *"grace"* (God's unmerited favor) *"through the redemption which is in Christ Jesus,"* a *"redemption"* that was applied once we exercised repentance and faith while depraved. No doubt, Jesus paid for our sins in 30 AD, but the payment was not credited to our account until we repented and believed while depraved.

As we examine the cross in greater depth, we will become increasingly aware of the Father's unfathomable love for us. Not only did He place our sins, along with the sins of all mankind, upon His selfless Son. He also established a friendship with us subsequent to our exercising repentance and faith while depraved. God's mercy demonstrated toward the repentant sinner is what *"propitiation"* is all about (Romans 3:25), for the same Greek word rendered *"propitiation"* in Romans 3:25 is rendered *"mercy seat"* in Hebrews 9:5. The mercy seat, positioned on top of the ark of the

> *Our sinful nature was eradicated through Christ's death.*

covenant in the tabernacle, and later in the temple, was where sins were atoned for, or covered. The high priest would enter the holy of holies *"...once a year... taking blood...for himself and for the sins of the people..."* (Hebrews 9:7). This blood was sprinkled on the mercy seat, after which the sins of Israel were covered. Jesus' death removed the need for this blood to be offered, a topic addressed in more depth in Hebrews 9:1-28.

Let me pose a question. How did the cross of Christ *"demonstrate"* God's *"righteousness"* (Romans 3:25)? In other words, was God right in judging sin? Of course He was, for He had to judge sin to remain just! He has never sinned, never will sin, and cannot condone sin. Since man is lost and incapable of saving himself, the only remedy was a sinless God-man who would die for sin. Because Jesus was without sin, He was the only Being who could die for man's misdeeds. He was the perfect offering. Indeed, God's *"righteousness,"* the fact that He was right in judging sin, was demonstrated on the cross.

This next topic is critical to comprehend if we are to view the cross from God's perspective, so meditate long and hard on what follows.

Sins were only atoned, or covered, through the sacrifices offered under the Mosaic Law. These sins were not forgiven until the cross. Consequently, no Old Testament believer's sins were forgiven until Jesus died. Thus Paul states:

> *...God...passed over the sins previously committed* (Romans 3:25).

Also, Hebrews 10:4 and 10:11 verify that *"the blood"* of animals could never *"take away sins."* Only the blood of Christ could accomplish such a feat.

Because God is *"...just and the justifier of the one who has faith in Jesus"* (v.26), the believer can take no credit for his salvation. Why so? All *"boasting...is excluded"* when we realize that we are *"justified by faith"* rather than by the *"works of the Law"* (vv.27-28). Don't misunderstand. Paul is not saying that the faith we exercised while depraved saved (justified) us, but rather that God saved (justified) us once we exercised faith while depraved. The faith we exercised while depraved, therefore, is not a work—the point that Paul is stressing in verses 27-28.

*P**aul is not saying that the faith we exercised while depraved saved (justified) us, but rather that God saved (justified) us once we exercised faith while depraved.***

Be sure to notice the phrase *"law of faith"* (v.27). The word *"law"* in this case, when viewed in context, can be translated "principle" and should not be confused with Law (rules and regulations). We are *"free"* from the Law of rules and regulations (Galatians 5:1) once we accept the *"law"* (principle) *"of faith"* (Romans 3:27). We will discuss this subject in more detail later.

According to Romans 3:29-30 and Ephesians 2, *"God"* is not only *"the God of Jews," "the circumcised,"* but He is also *"the God of Gentiles," "the uncircumcised."* In fact, Ephesians 2:14 states that Jesus *"made both groups into one."* Thus, during the church age, both Jews and Gentiles become *"one body"* through being placed in Christ subsequent to repenting and believing while depraved. Note Paul's words from Ephesians 2:14-16:

> *For He Himself is our peace, who made both groups into one, and broke down*
> *the barrier of the dividing wall, by abolishing in His flesh the enmity, which is*
> *the Law of commandments contained in ordinances, that in Himself He might*
> *make the two into one new man, thus establishing peace, and might reconcile*
> *them both in one body to God through the cross, by it having put to death the*
> *enmity.* (Ephesians 2:14-16)

Undeniably, repentance and faith must be exercised by the depraved before God will award salvation. Paul is not teaching, therefore, that the repentance and faith exercised by the depraved saves (justifies) them. Rather, he is teaching that God saves (justifies) the depraved once they exercise repentance and faith. In this case, does our *"faith"* in any way *"nullify the Law"*? Paul says it does not in Romans 3:31:

> *Do we then nullify the Law through faith? May it never be! On the contrary, we*
> *establish the Law.* (Romans 3:31)

We must remember the initial purpose of the Law to follow Paul's line of thinking, for it was given to expose sin (Romans 3:19-20) and to show man his need for a Savior (Galatians 3:24). Thus, we do not *"nullify the Law through faith"* but *"establish"* it (Romans 3:31). Isn't this fun?!

Romans 4:1-12 Questions

First Day

1.   Read Romans 4:1-12. Why would Paul mention Abraham at this point in his epistle? What position did Abraham hold in the Jewish nation?

2.   Read Genesis 12:1-15:21 and record what you discover regarding Abraham's faith.

Second Day

1.   Read Romans 4:1-12. Continue to read about Abraham in Genesis 16:1 through 19:38. Write down all you find that relates to Abraham's faith.

Third Day

1.   Read Romans 4:1-12. Also read Genesis 20:1 through 22:24. Could you display the type of faith that Abraham exemplified in these chapters? If not, what positive steps can you take to possess a similar faith?

2.   Now that you have read Genesis 12:1 through 22:24, list some of Abraham's weaknesses.

3.   Abraham was viewed as a man of faith even with his many weaknesses (read Hebrews 11:8-12). Did you notice that none of Abraham's character flaws are mentioned in Hebrews 11:8-12? What does this say regarding our God?

Fourth Day

1.   Read Romans 4:1-12. According to Hebrews 11:17-19, what was Abraham thinking and believing as he offered up Isaac? What does this tell you about the importance of knowing God's *"promises"* and believing God's *"promises"* as Abraham did?

2.   What does Paul say about Abraham in Romans 4:1-3? How do verses 2-3 verify that faith, exercised while depraved, nullifies boasting? Note how Romans 4:2-3 and Romans 3:27 support each other, teaching that the faith exercised by the depraved, prior to spiritual regeneration, is not a work.

3.   According to verse 3, what caused God to reckon (count) Abraham as righteous? Do you remember which verse in Genesis 15 speaks of this wonderful event? Remember the address of this passage, for it will serve you well as we progress.

Fifth Day

1.   Read Romans 4:1-12. What does verse 4 communicate to you? According to verse 5, is the *"faith"* exercised by the lost (depraved) a work?

2.   In Romans 4:5, Paul writes that God *"justifies the ungodly."* Who are *"the ungodly"*?

3.   *"David"* is mentioned in Romans 4:6 and quoted in verses 7 and 8. He speaks of a particular *"blessing."* What is that *"blessing"*? From what we have studied thus far, how is this *"blessing"* received?

Sixth Day

1.   Read Romans 4:1-12. Do you remember which verse in Genesis 15 speaks of Abraham being declared righteous? Once you have found this passage, read Genesis 17:22-24. Was Abraham declared righteous before or after he was circumcised? How does this tie in with Romans 4:9-11. Write down any new insights.

2.   According to Romans 4:11-12, what is the purpose of circumcision? Now, in your own words, write down the purpose of circumcision.

Romans 4:1-12 Lesson

Abraham's Faith Apart from Works

In this section, Paul brings up one of the great names in history: Abraham. What you studied this week should have confirmed that Abraham was a man of faith. He obeyed God and moved from Haran to Canaan (Genesis 12:1-5). He also believed God's promises (Genesis 15:6), after which, through obedience, he circumcised his entire household (Genesis 17:9-27). Even Abraham himself was circumcised according to Genesis 17:24. Plus, when asked by God to do so, he offered up Isaac, the son of promise, on the altar (Genesis 22:1-19). Abraham could respond in this manner for one reason only: God had promised that Isaac would have descendants (Genesis 17:19, 21:12). He knew, therefore, that God would resurrect Isaac should he (Abraham) take Isaac's life (Hebrews 11:17-19). Can you see the importance of knowing God's promises? Doesn't this encourage you to know God's Word?!

No doubt, Abraham possessed tremendous faith. But he also, like us, possessed weaknesses. He asked Sarah to lie about their relationship as husband and wife and pose as his sister. He did this twice, in Genesis 12:10-20 and Genesis 20. She was, in actuality, his half-sister (Genesis 20:12), but God hates half-truths because half-truths are sin. Sarah was supernaturally protected, however, due to God's promises.

Even though Abraham possessed great faith, he possessed character flaws that only God could mend. For instance, instead of waiting for Sarah to conceive and bear the son of promise, he became impatient and Ishmael was born through Hagar (Genesis 16). Yet, notice that God mentions none of his sins in Hebrews 11:8-12 and 17-19. If you have submitted to the God of Abraham, He has wiped your slate clean as well!!

To the Jews, none is greater than Abraham; he is their father (Romans 4:1; John 8:37-39). How then do Jews, being descendants of Abraham, obtain a righteous standing before God? The answer is embedded in Romans 4.

Had Abraham been *"...justified by works, he has something to boast about..."* (v.2). We have already studied, however, that no one can work his way into a right standing with God. Consequently, Abraham's faith, exercised while depraved, caused God to reckon (count) him as righteous (Romans 4:3).

If you have submitted to the God of Abraham, He has wiped your slate clean as well!

Do you understand what Paul is saying in Romans 4:4? So long as we perceive our good works as gaining points with God, we may wrongly view God as owing us something. Unless this attitude is replaced with repentance and *"faith"* (Romans 4:5), the holder will face God's judgment of Revelation 20:11-15.

Notice too that God is in the business of justifying *"the ungodly"* (Romans 4:5). Before God will make us righteous, we must acknowledge while depraved that we are *"ungodly"*—totally and completely shipwrecked in regard to righteousness and holiness. This *"repentance,"* a change of attitude concerning sin, *"leads to life"* (Acts 11:18), the eternal *"life"* that God gives to the depraved who choose to repent and believe.

In Romans 4:6, Paul speaks of David, the man after God's own heart, the man beloved of God. Paul's point here, when taken through all of the Scriptures, is that David believed that God's *"righteousness"* is bestowed (apart from the works of the Law) upon those who exercise repentance and faith while depraved. In fact, these passages prove that the Lord does not *"take"* a New Testament believer's *"sin...into account"* (vv.7-8). Thus, God has no record of any sin we have committed in the past. Neither does He record any sin we commit in the present or future. We will discuss this further in a few weeks.

Abraham's Faith Apart from Circumcision

In Romans 4:9-10, Paul brings circumcision back into the picture for a good reason. He wants to prove that God declared Abraham righteous before Abraham was circumcised. By making his case from the Scriptures alone, he removes the Jews' ability to say that Abraham was declared righteous because of circumcision. Observe as Paul develops his argument.

First, in Romans 4:9 he asks the Jews if the *"blessing"* mentioned by David in Romans 4:7-8 is *"...upon the circumcised, or upon the uncircumcised also..."* Then he again references Abraham, because it was through Abraham that the covenant of circumcision was instituted (Genesis 17:9-27). Next, in Romans 4:10, Paul asks if Abraham was declared righteous by God before or after he was *"circumcised."* To answer this question, the Jews would have consulted the book of Genesis and discovered that Abraham was declared righteous in Genesis 15:6, at least thirteen years before he was circumcised (read Genesis 15:6; 16:16; 17:24). Therefore, the uncircumcised can be declared righteous, proving that circumcision guarantees no one a right standing before God. As usual, Paul proves his point!

Romans 4:11 explains the purpose of *"circumcision,"* for it is both a *"sign"* and *"a seal."* How is it a *"sign"*? Every time a Jew sees someone circumcised, or is reminded of his own circumcision, he is to remember that God bestows righteousness on the basis of *"faith."* It is *"a seal"* because it cannot be undone. It proves, in other words, that once God makes us righteous, subsequent to our exercising repentance and faith while depraved, we cannot lose our righteousness and become unrighteous. The same principle applied in Paul's day as well. In fact, it applied to believers who lived before the cross, although they were only <u>declared</u> righteous prior to Jesus' perfect sacrifice. The great news is that they were <u>made</u> righteous through Jesus' death, burial, and resurrection. If this is somewhat confusing, it won't be later on. This subject will be addressed in great depth in the weeks ahead.

Did you notice that Abraham is *"the father of all who believe"* (vv.11-12), whether they are physically circumcised or not? This truth verifies that Jews and Gentiles alike become descendants of Abraham through faith. In other words, they become true Jews (Romans 2:28-29). Paul addresses this subject in Ephesians 2:11-16, where he states that *"both groups,"* believing Jews and Gentiles alike during the church age, are *"made...into one"* (v.14). Consequently, through faith, and God's resulting salvation, Jews and Gentiles partake of the "spiritual" blessings promised to Abraham.

> *O*nce God makes us righteous, subsequent to our exercising repentance and faith while depraved, we cannot lose our righteousness and become unrighteous.

Don't misunderstand. God continues to deal with the physical Jewish nation as a separate nation, as He has done since Genesis 12—when He began making promises to Abraham. He, therefore, will fulfill the physical and spiritual promises He made to physical Israel (review the lesson associated with Week 2).

Are you seeing how man can misinterpret God's purpose and plan? God's purpose in having man circumcised was pure and wholesome, yet man misunderstood it and suffered the consequence of his error. Are we not guilty of the same as we mishandle the truth associated with the gospel? Oh, if we could but perceive truth as God perceives truth! This clarity should be our goal as we continue, no matter the cost.

Romans 4:13-25 Questions

Previous lessons should be of great value as we work through this week's questions and lesson. Remember to pray for wisdom.

First Day

1. Read Romans 4:13-25. According to Romans 4:13, what *"promise"* did God make to Abraham? Did the Law given to Moses come into existence before or after this *"promise"?*

2. According to Galatians 3:15-18, by how many years did God's *"promise"* to Abraham precede His giving of *"the Law"* to Israel through Moses? Relate your answer to Paul's statement in Romans 4:14 and record what you find.

3. Take some time to thank the Lord for delivering you from Law and placing you under grace subsequent to your choice to repent and believe while depraved.

Second Day

1. Read Romans 4:13-25. What does Paul mean when he says, *"for the Law brings about wrath..."* (v.15)? Tie this in with Romans 3:19-20.

2. What does Paul mean when he says, *"...where there is no law, neither is there violation"* (v.15)? Did God not count man's sin against man prior to giving the Law to Israel? Explain. I realize that this may be a difficult question, but give it your best shot. This week's lesson should help if you need assistance.

Third Day

1. Read Romans 4:13-25. In verses 16 and 17, Paul explains why God bestows righteousness on the basis of *"faith"* rather than *"Law."* What is the reason?

2. Tie Galatians 3:7 and 29 into your previous answer.

3. How is God described in Romans 4:17? What does the phrase, *"...calls into being that which does not exist,"* communicate to you about God? Read Hebrews 11:3 and Ephesians 3:20 to see how they relate to what we have just studied.

4. When was the last time the Lord met your need by calling something *"into being"* which did not previously *"exist"?*

Fourth Day

1. Read Romans 4:13-25. Now read Romans 4:18 a second time. What does it mean to *"hope against hope"?* Have you done this at any time in the past? If so, how did you continue to carry on when your circumstances appeared to be so hopeless? What did God teach you about Himself through this experience? List some verses (promises) that encouraged you as you walked in this manner?

Fifth Day

1. Read Romans 4:13-25. To what did Abraham hold that allowed him to *"hope against hope"* (vv.18-21)? What does this communicate regarding Abraham's perception of God's promises?

2. Since the phrase, *"giving glory to God,"* refers to praise, verse 20 grants insight into the connection between praise and faith. In Abraham's life, how were they related? Have they been related in the same manner in your own experience? Explain.

3. Read part or all of Psalm 145-150 and record what you discover regarding praise.

Sixth Day

1. Read Romans 4:13-25. In Romans 4:22, Paul states that Abraham was *"reckoned"* as righteous before God. What did Abraham believe that caused God to reckon (declare) him as righteous? For the correct answer, remember what we studied in the previous verses.

2. What must we believe for God to reckon us as righteous (vv.23-24)? Note: We must be careful to interpret the word *"reckoned,"* as it relates to righteousness, in its proper context. Old Testament believers were only <u>declared</u> righteous when they exercised repentance and faith while depraved, but were <u>made</u> righteous when Jesus died. In other words, they were saved on credit. New Testament believers, on the other hand, are <u>made</u> righteous the moment they repent and believe while depraved. Therefore, when the word *"reckoned"* is used in association with righteousness, be careful to remember this truth.

3. What does Romans 4:25 communicate regarding the death and resurrection of Jesus Christ?

4. What is the most encouraging truth that you take away from this week's questions?

Romans 4:13-25 Lesson

Abraham's Faith Apart from Law

This week, we have continued our study of Abraham, the man of faith. In Romans 4:9-12, Paul uses Abraham to prove that physical circumcision has nothing to do with making man right with God. In Romans 4:13-25, he again refers to Abraham, this time to illustrate that righteousness, a right standing with God, is unattainable through the works of the Law.

God promised Abraham *"...that he would be heir of the world..."* (Romans 4:13). You may ask, "Where did God make such a promise?" The answer is found in Genesis 17:4-6 and again in Genesis 22:17. Later in today's lesson, we will study the details of this promise. But for now, note that the promise was made prior to the issuing of the Law: The promise coming in the book of Genesis, the Law being issued later in the book of Exodus.

Do you see Paul's point? Many Jews had believed the lie that the Law was their ticket to heaven. Paul proves the error in their thinking, for God's *"promise"* to Abraham came some *"four hundred and thirty years"* before the Law (Galatians 3:17). Therefore, *"...if those who are of the Law are heirs, faith is made void and the promise* [given to Abraham] *is nullified"* (Romans 4:14). Thus, Paul again proves that the Law cannot save.

The reason the Law cannot save is because *"...the Law brings about wrath..."* (Romans 4:15). The Law was given to shut our mouths (Romans 3:19) and show us our need for a Savior (Galatians 3:24). No one will ever be saved by keeping the Law (Romans 3:20), for its purpose is to reveal man's need for Christ. Anyone who declines to acknowledge this need and refuses to exercise repentance and faith while depraved will be condemned at the *"great white throne"* judgment of Revelation 20:11-15. No doubt, *"...the Law brings about wrath..."* (Romans 4:15).

> *M*any Jews had believed the lie that the Law was their ticket to heaven.

The latter part of Romans 4:15 is extremely interesting: *"...but where there is no law, neither is there violation."* Is Paul teaching that sin was not judged prior to the Law (the Law given to Moses)? No way! The Law was given in Exodus 20, yet sin was judged many times between Genesis 1:1 and Exodus 20. This judgment resulted because man lived under moral law even before the time of the Mosaic Law. So what is Paul communicating here? He is saying that the Law was given to increase the lost man's awareness that he is in violation of God's standard for holiness. Paul emphasizes this point in Galatians 3:24, where he states that *"the Law"* was given as a *"tutor to lead us to Christ."* The Law's main purpose is to show the lost (depraved) that they need a Savior and are living a life of *"violation"* (Romans 4:15).

Abraham's Faith in the "Seed" (Christ)

The story doesn't end here. God saves the lost (depraved), once they exercise *"faith"* (and repentance, of course), in order that salvation might be presented to mankind on the basis of His *"grace"* (Romans 4:16). By doing so, He can offer salvation to everyone—not just the recipients of the Law. In fact, God makes a person a spiritual descendant of Abraham once repentance and faith are exercised —regardless of that person's nationality (Romans 4:16-17). Follow how this works.

"Christ" is Abraham's *"seed"* (Galatians 3:16):

Now the promises were spoken to Abraham and to his seed. He does not say,
"And to seeds," as referring to many, but rather to one, "And to your seed,"that
is, Christ. (Galatians 3:16)

When a person during the church age exercises faith in Christ (while depraved), he is placed *"in Christ"* and made *"new"* (2 Corinthians 5:17):

Therefore if any man is in Christ, he is a new creature; the old things passed
away; behold, new things have come. (2Corinthians 5:17)

Once *"in Christ,"* that individual, regardless of nationality, is Abraham's spiritual descendant (Galatians 3:7 and 29). After all, the book of Galatians was written to Gentiles:

Therefore, be sure that it is those who are of faith who are sons of Abraham.
(Galatians 3:7)

And if you belong to Christ, then you are Abraham's offspring, heirs according to
promise. (Galatians 3:29)

Abraham is the father of many nations because all believers from Acts 2 (the beginning of the church age) through the Rapture become a member of the body of Christ, the church, through being placed in Christ the moment they exercise repentance and faith while depraved. We will discuss how the New Testament believer is placed in Christ later in the course.

Do you realize that *"...God...gives life to the dead and calls into being that which does not exist"* (Romans 4:17)? According to Romans 4:18-21, God met Abraham's need through responding in this more than miraculous manner. No doubt, God spoke the world into existence, *"...so that what is seen was not made out of things which are visible"* (Hebrews 11:3). But some may ask, "Does He function in the same fashion today?" You bet He does, for many believers walk in the realm of the miraculous at this very moment! By consistently yielding the Christ's life, no mountain is too high to climb, no valley is too low to cross, and no problem is too difficult for God to resolve. God is perceived as the God in charge, the God Who is capable of performing the impossible regardless of the circumstance. How does God accomplish these feats? He does so by merely speaking a word. Truly, nothing is more exhilarating than the life of faith.

We need to remember what is discussed here, for much of what we will experience as a believer is described in the first phrase of Romans 4:18. Abraham knew how to *"hope against hope,"* and so must we. To *"hope against hope"* means to *"hope"* when there is no logical reason to *"hope."* When God is perceived as capable of speaking into existence that which we need, we can continue to *"hope."* Abraham continued to *"hope"* because of God's promise. As a result, God did the impossible, giving Abraham a son in the midst of incredible circumstances (Romans 4:19-20). He will allow the impossible to occur in our lives as well if we will but rest in His promises. It is imperative, therefore, that we know what He has promised! Where are His promises found? They are found in His letter to man! Need I say more?!

The last phrase of Romans 4:20 is an extremely powerful statement! It says that Abraham *"...grew strong in faith, giving glory to God."* Abraham's faith was enlarged as a result of praise, which verifies that praise is the fuel for faith. We can't read Psalms 145-150, Psalms of praise, without witnessing the value of worship. Praise energizes faith by restoring the worshippers' perception of Who God is—the One and Only Sovereign of the universe. When God is perceived in this light, His promises are easily appropriated. I am not saying that praise is always easy, for Hebrews 13:15 states that we are to *"...continually offer up a sacrifice of praise to God…"* No doubt, praise can be *"a sacrifice."* But praise always empowers faith to the glory of God.

Praise always empowers faith to the glory of God.

In Romans 4:22, Paul again emphasizes that God *"reckoned"* (counted) Abraham as righteous due to Abraham's faith. (Remember that Abraham was declared righteous in Genesis 15:6 <u>before</u> he was made righteous through Jesus' death.) According to Romans 4:23-24, every person during the church age who exercises faith in Christ receives this same righteousness. No Jew could say, therefore, that anything but faith coupled with repentance could cause God to make man righteous. Paul has proven his point and proven it well. (Have you noticed the degree to which Paul repeats himself? Every good teacher realizes the importance of hammering home his point.)

The last verse in this chapter speaks of the death and resurrection of Christ along with the purpose of each. Jesus *"…was delivered up because of our transgressions, and was raised because of our justification"* (Romans 4:25). The fact that Jesus died for our *"transgressions"* is undeniable. Isn't it wonderful to know that everything needed for *"our justification,"* *"justification"* being God's gift to those who repent and believe while depraved, was also provided through the cross? Had this not been the case, Jesus would have remained in the grave—*"He…was raised because of our justification."* This verse will become more meaningful when we study Romans 5-8.

As we move into Romans 5 and discuss justification in detail, be prepared to experience some of the most exciting Scripture in the entire Word of God.

Romans 5:1 Questions

Concerning Justification

First Day

1.   Read Romans 5:1 and review the two lessons (lessons only—not questions) associated with Romans 4 (Weeks 5 and 6). Why would Paul begin Romans 5:1 with the word *"Therefore"?* According to verse 1, how is a person *"justified"?*

2.   How does the truth you learned in Romans 4 tie in with the fact that God justified us on the basis of our own personal faith (and repentance, of course) exercised while depraved (Romans 5:1)?

3.   Take some time to think about the word *"justified."* Now try to define it.

Second Day

1.   Read Romans 5:1. The remainder of this week you will study verses that describe the person whom God has justified. As you proceed, remember that God justifies us the instant we accept Christ as Savior. Write down what each verse says about the person whom the Father has justified: 2 Corinthians 5:17; Galatians 2:20; 2 Corinthians 5:21; Romans 8:1; Ephesians 1:13; 1:4; 2:6. Meditate on these verses, and ask God to open the eyes of your heart for understanding (Ephesians 1:18).

Third Day

1.   Read and try to memorize Romans 5:1. Study the following verses, and continue to record what results when we are justified: Colossians 3:1, 3, 13; Ephesians 4:32; Colossians 2:13; Romans 8:30; Romans 6:6; Colossians 3:9-10; Ephesians 4:22-24.

Fourth Day

1.   Read Romans 5:1. Continue to study the results of justification by reading the following verses. Write down what you find: Hebrews 9:28; 10.10, 10:14; Ephesians 5:30; Colossians 1:22; 2:10; 1Corinthians 1:30.

Fifth Day

1.   Read Romans 5:1. Study the following verses and continue to write down what results when we are justified: 1 Corinthians 1:2, 8; 6:11; Ephesians 2:19; Philippians 3:20; Colossians 2:12; 3:12.

Sixth Day

1.   Read Romans 5:1. Two more verses, 1John 5:20 and Jude 1, and we are finished. Study them and write down what you learn about the person who is justified.

2.   How has this week's lesson encouraged you? Do you have trouble accepting the fact that everything you studied for the past five days happened at the point of justification? If so, why?

Romans 5:1 Lesson

Justification by Faith

Are you ready to consider a utterly fascinating dimension of the Christian life? In this section, we will discover that Jesus did more than get us out of hell and into heaven. His obedience, coupled with the faith and repentance God requires from the depraved, is what caused the Father to justify us! He made us not guilty by saving us through His Son. He did it in an instant of time, the instant we, while lost and depraved, realized our need for a Savior, repented of our sins, and asked Jesus Christ into our hearts through faith. This news is more than good! It is life!

Justification was defined earlier as "just as if I never sinned or ever will sin again." God, in a moment's time, ushered us out of a state of condemnation (Ephesians 2:1-3) and made us righteous (right) before Him. He did it on the basis of our own personal repentance and faith exercised while we were depraved! Paul speaks of this astounding transformation in Romans 5:1:

> *Therefore having been justified by faith, we have peace with God through our*
> *Lord Jesus Christ,* (Romans 5:1)

At the outset, consider a significant point regarding the phrase, *"having been justified by faith."* Paul, by no stretch of the imagination, is teaching that *"faith"* saves. *"Faith"* has never saved anyone. God does the saving. Man does the believing. Thus, *"faith,"* exercised by the depraved, cannot be classified as a work—as verified by previous lessons. This truth will be confirmed to a greater degree as we continue, so prepare yourself. We will be digging extremely deep.

God, in a moment's time, ushered us out of a state of condemnation and made us righteous (right) before Him.

Notice that the first word in Romans 5 is *"Therefore."* Paul makes use of this term because it took the first four chapters of this epistle to prove that God bestows righteousness upon those who repent and believe while depraved. Consequently, we were *"justified"* by God as a result of exercising faith <u>prior</u> to being born again! Yes, God saves; man believes. Man in his lost (depraved) state must believe, however, before God will save. We also studied last week that *"...it* [the salvation that comes through God alone] *is by faith, that it might be in accordance with grace..."* (Romans 4:16). Thus, justification is available to man solely as a result of God's grace.

I view justification in this manner:

> Several years ago, in the midst of my depravity, I saw my need for a Savior (repented, in other words) and exercised personal faith. I did this by looking to heaven and saying, "God help, I need a Savior." God then did all the rest. Much more occurred than initially meets the eye, so let me attempt to explain by offering the following illustration:
>
> When I gave my life to Christ (when I exercised personal repentance and faith while depraved), God, seated in heaven behind His huge gold desk, took His huge gold gavel (no desk or gavel are mentioned in Scripture—again, this is an illustration), stood up behind His desk, raised up on His tip-toes, and with all the force that He could muster through that right arm of power, struck that huge, gold, glistening desk. As a result of this act, all heaven shook—even the angels took notice—and every eye in the heavenly places gazed at the Creator. As He prepared to speak, they could not help but notice the love and compassion that characterized His stature. As they gazed more intently, they could see tears of

joy rushing down those cheeks from which the glory of His Majesty was manifested. Then, when everything in heaven had settled, the Creator pointed at me. Here is where our illustration ends and Scriptural reality kicks in, although some of what is stated above may very well have occurred:

With great boldness and authority, and yet with great joy, my God said this about me: "You are holy, perfect, redeemed, complete, blameless, accepted, glorified, a brother of Christ, not condemned, a saint, a son, forgiven, and I take you as my very own!"

Wow! Can you believe that the Father did all of that (and more) in an instant of time? This entire transformation occurred at the point of justification, subsequent to our exercising repentance and faith while depraved. God did it all through His grace!

Let's observe a few New Testament verses that confirm what has been stated regarding justification. The verse reference is listed on the left. What God says about us in each verse is listed on the right. Keep in mind that everything addressed here happened in an instant, at the point of justification. Turn the page and bask in the greatness of what you find.

What Happened at the Point of Justification:

A Description of the New Testament Believer—The New Man (New Self)

2 Corinthians 5:17 .... New Creation

Galatians 2:20 .... Crucified With Christ - Christ Lives In Me!

2 Corinthians 5:21 .... Righteousness Of God

Romans 8:1 .... Not Condemned

Ephesians 1:13 .... Sealed In Him (Secure)

Ephesians 1:4 .... Holy And Blameless Before Him

Ephesians 2:6 .... Seated In The Heavenly Places

Colossians 3:1 .... Raised Up With Christ

Colossians 3:3 .... Have Died — Our Life Is Hidden With Christ In God!

Colossians 3:13 .... Forgiven

Ephesians 4:32 .... Forgiven

Colossians 2:13 .... Forgiven

Romans 8:30 .... Justified, Glorified

Romans 6:6 .... Old Self (Adamic Nature) Was Crucified

Colossians 3:9,10 .... Laid Aside Old Self, Put On New Self

Ephesians 4:22-24 .... Laid Aside Old Self, Put On New Self

Hebrews 10:10 .... Sanctified

Hebrews 10:14 .... Perfected

Hebrews 9:28 .... Forgiven

Ephesians 5:30 .... Members Of His Body

Colossians 1:22 .... Holy, Blameless, And Beyond Reproach

Colossians 2:10 .... Complete

1 Corinthians 1:30 .... In Christ, Righteous, Sanctified, Redeemed

1 Corinthians 1:2 .... Made Us Into A Saint

1 Corinthians 1:8 .... Confirmed To The End, Blameless

1 Corinthians 6:11 .... Washed, Sanctified, Justified

Ephesians 2:19 .... Member Of God's Household

Philippians 3:20 .... Citizenship In Heaven

Colossians 3:12 .... Holy And Beloved

Colossians 2:12 .... Buried With Him

1 John 5:20 .... In Christ

Jude 1 .... Kept For Jesus Christ

Everything listed in the previous thirty-two verses pertains to the New Testament believer who, while depraved, repented and exercised personal faith. Can you see why the gospel is called *The Good News?* This truth is not "positional" truth, as some have incorrectly assumed. It is much more. It is reality! "Positional Truth," which is taught in many Christian circles, is misleading. It carries with it the idea that God somehow <u>sees</u> us in the manner that these verses describe us—but in actuality we are just lowly sinners saved by grace, who will someday (in heaven) become all of these things. Scripture presents a totally different view, for we are <u>now</u> (present tense) everything these thirty-two verses say about us? We can *"rest"*—and more. The evidence is in the tenses of the verbs used in these passages. The action is past tense action, action that occurred when we met Jesus. Therefore, we are <u>now</u> holy, perfect, righteous, complete, etc.—not lowly sinners saved by grace. In fact, we are saints who sometimes sin! Can you see the difference in these two perspectives? Pray that God will enlighten your spiritual eyes so you might perceive yourself as He sees you.

God's view of us means that He is not required to look at us through Jesus to "stomach" what He sees. The Father loves us because of who we are—because of what He has made us into. He isn't required, as I supposed as a new believer, to view us through His peripheral vision due to a lowliness we possess as His sons. He can look at us straight on because of what He made us into at the point of justification, for He accepts us and desires that we know His heart. As a result, He is accessible, ready to listen to our every concern, and ready to defend us to the very end—because of who we are—because of what He made us into subsequent to our exercising repentance and faith while depraved.

The writer of Hebrews verifies, beyond doubt, that *"There remains...a Sabbath rest for the people of God"* (Hebrews 4:9). Why can New Testament believers *"rest"*? We can *"rest"* because God, in an instant of time, made us into the most holy and righteous beings imaginable. The work is a finished work. We are blameless before Him. We are also set free to enjoy, for all eternity, all that Christ has done for the redeemed.

Because we are blameless and free, our focus should center on knowing—really *KNOWING*—Christ and yielding to His indwelling presence (Philippians 3:10; Galatians 2:20). When we do so, we are

> *God, in an instant of time, made us into the most holy and righteous beings imaginable.*

"filled" with God's Spirit (Ephesians 5:18), and those around us cannot help but see Jesus. Thus, we *"rest"* as God lives His holy and omnipotent life through us. What a deal!

With this backdrop, we can understand why Paul stated that *"...neither circumcision nor uncircumcision means anything, but faith working through love"* (Galatians 5:6). Did you catch that? Love, not duty, causes us to yearn to live by faith, to live a life characterized by trust in the Creator. Yes, what God did for us at the point of justification not only revolutionizes our perception of who we are, but also revolutionizes our perception of who He is. When this revolution occurs, everything about our lives is invigorated, not by our own energy, but by His, as we yield to His indwelling presence. Interested in learning more? If so, you should enjoy what lies ahead.

Before leaving this section, we need additional input regarding the subject of *"faith"* (Romans 5:1). No doubt, faith and repentance are highly debated topics in our day. In fact, they have been debated for centuries. As a result, the following should be read intensely.

The Contextual View of Repentance and Faith

The Scriptures teach that God does the saving and man does the repenting and believing, for God saves those who exercise repentance and faith. A debate exists, however, regarding the source of this repentance and faith. In fact, at least two schools of thought exist within Christendom: (1) Repentance and faith are God's gifts to those who will subsequently believe and be saved (2) Repentance and faith originate with the depraved (the spiritually unregenerated) and are exercised prior to God bestowing salvation.

The first school (1) views the depraved (the spiritually unregenerated) as totally incapable of exercising personal repentance and faith. In fact, they view the depraved as spiritual corpses—unable to respond to any spiritual stimulus. Therefore, they view the depravity of man as being a Total Depravity—thus the "T" of the TULIP.

The remaining letters of the acrostic (ULIP) naturally follow, for they rest on the foundation of this extreme view of depravity. Under this arrangement, God must, by means of Unconditional Election (the "U" of the TULIP), elect (choose) each family member from eternity past by means of an eternal decree. Why? Based on this view, the depraved are incapable of repenting and believing due to their spiritual deadness. Hence, God must make that choice for them.

What naturally follows is Limited Atonement (the "L" of the TULIP)—a mindset that views Jesus as dying for the elect alone. Any of His blood shed for the non-elect would be wasted according to this view.

The next letter of the TULIP (the "I") must logically (not scripturally) follow. After all, if the depraved are incapable of exercising personal repentance and faith, as is incorrectly assumed, God must, through Irresistible Grace (the "I"), draw the elect to Himself when it is their time to believe. Thus, the following sequence is incorrectly assumed: (1) God must spiritually regenerate the depraved prior to salvation (2) God follows by awarding the spiritually regenerated the gifts of repentance and faith (3) The spiritually regenerated who have received God's gifts of repentance and faith then repent, believe, and are saved. This arrangement is unacceptable, for to be spiritually regenerated is equivalent to being saved. So, according to this sequence, the believer is saved twice—a direct violation of the Scriptures.

This school also requires the elect to persevere for the purpose of proving that they have been elected. Thus, the "P" of the TULIP, Perseverance of the Saints. Is it any wonder that many who believe in the TULIP lack assurance of their salvation? After all, to what degree must one persevere to validate his election? The answer is unattainable due to the unscriptural nature of this system of thought.

*B*ecause the TULIP rests upon the foundation of the "T," Total Depravity, it rests upon shaky ground.

Because the TULIP rests upon the foundation of the "T," Total Depravity, it rests upon shaky ground. Numerous Scriptures confirm that the depraved can recognize their lost state and, in turn, understand their need for a Savior. Adam and Eve are prime examples, for after sinning and becoming depraved *"...they knew that they were naked..."* (Genesis 3:7). Thus, *"...they sewed fig leaves together..."* to cover themselves due to their sin:

Then the eyes of both of them were opened, and they knew that they were naked; and they sewed fig leaves together and made themselves loin coverings. (Genesis 3:7)

Also realize that Philippians 2:11 states:

*that at the name of Jesus EVERY KNEE SHOULD BOW, of those who are in heaven,
and on earth, and under the earth, and that every tongue should confess that
Jesus Christ is Lord, to the glory of God the Father.* (Philippians 2:10-11)

Many who *"bow"* in this instance and *"confess that Jesus is Lord"* will be depraved (spiritually unregenerated), for *"every knee"* of mankind will *"bow"* instead of just some. The depraved will respond in this manner, obviously, without being spiritually regenerated—negating the "T" of the TULIP, along with the other letters of the acrostic (ULIP), altogether.

No doubt, it is absolutely critical that the subjects of repentance and faith be perceived from a Scriptural basis. We will begin our discussion by addressing Ephesians 2:8-9:

*For by grace you have been saved through faith; and that not of yourselves, it is
the gift of God; not as a result of works, that no one should boast.* (Ephesians
2:8-9)

Paul emphasizes that salvation is most definitely by God's *"grace"* (read Romans 3:24 and Titus 3:7 as well). Paul also affirms that *"...the righteous man shall live by faith"* (Romans 1:17), a quote from Habakkuk 2:4.

The word *"that"* in the phrase, *"and that not of yourselves"* (Ephesians 2:8), is a major source of contention between (1) Those who view faith as God's gift and (2) Those who perceive faith as originating with the depraved (the spiritually unregenerated—the lost). Those in the first camp view *"that"* as pointing to *"faith."* The second camp views *"that"* as pointing to *"saved."* Which is correct? It is a necessity that we answer this question properly, so enjoy what follows.

If you are unfamiliar with the Greek language, the subsequent sentence will sound like "Greek," but is much needed input. The word *"that"* (in Ephesians 2:8) refers to *"saved"* because *"faith"* is a feminine noun, while the demonstrative pronoun *"that"* is neuter, making it impossible for *"that"* to refer to *"faith."* Alford, F. F. Bruce, A. T. Robertson, W. E. Vine, Scofield, and additional Greek authorities would agree according Dave Hunt, in *What Love Is This?*, page 452.[i] In addition, we find the following in the margin of the New American Standard Bible regarding *"that"* in Ephesians 2:8:

I.e., that salvation

Ephesians 2:9, when coupled with Ephesians 2:8, also confirms that *salvation*, not *"faith,"* is the *"gift."* Note how Ephesians 2:9 applies:

not as a result of works, that no one should boast. (Ephesians 2:9)

Paul is teaching that salvation (*"saved"*—Ephesians 2:8) is *"not...a result of works..."* (Ephesians 2:9). Salvation is a *"gift"* (Ephesians 2:8) received by those who exercise *"faith"* (Ephesians 2:8) while depraved. Thus, it is impossible to work yourself into a right standing with God. This truth is exactly what Paul teaches elsewhere. Read Romans 3:27-28, for example, realizing that *"justified"* points to salvation:

*Where then is boasting? It is excluded. By what kind of law? Of works? No, but
by a law of faith. For we maintain that a man is <u>justified by faith apart from
works of the Law</u>.* (Romans 3:27-28)

Paul proves once again that we are *"justified"* (saved) *"apart from works"* (Romans 3:28). This is the identical truth that he conveys in Ephesians 2:8-9. Paul also confirms that *"boasting"* is *"excluded"* in such cases (Romans 3:27). Thus, to exercise *"faith"* while depraved is <u>not</u> a work. In fact, Paul contrasts *"faith"* with *"works"* on many occasions in the Scriptures. Consequently, choosing to exercise personal *"faith"* in the midst of one's depravity is <u>not</u> a meritorious deed. Paul teaches the same principle in Romans 4:5, contrasting *"work"* with believing:

> *But to the one who <u>does not work, but believes</u> in Him who justifies the ungodly, his faith is reckoned as righteousness,* (Romans 4:5)

Romans 9:30-32 confirms the same truth:

> *What shall we say then? That Gentiles, who did not pursue righteousness, attained righteousness, even the righteousness which is by faith; but Israel, pursuing a law of righteousness, did not arrive at that law. Why? <u>Because they did not pursue it by faith, but as though it were by works</u>...* (Romans 9:30-32)

Scripture has a great deal more to say about *"faith."* We have already determined that *"faith"* (Ephesians 2:8-9) originates within the heart of the depraved (also read Acts 16:31, Acts 26:18, and Romans 10:8-10). It is not God's gift, for *"faith"* springs forth from the lost (the depraved—the spiritually unregenerated) who desire to be saved. I exercised faith in my depravity when I said, "God help, I need a Savior." In that statement, I exhibited not only faith, but repentance as well (we will address repentance shortly). Thus, faith was not the Father's gift prior to His saving me. On the other hand, we must not overlook the Father's drawing (John 6:44) and the Spirit's conviction (John 16:8) that have been ever-present in our lives. But the faith we exercised prior to salvation was our own faith, initiated in our depravity. It was not the Father's gift!

For sure, the *"faith"* addressed in Ephesians 2:8-9 cannot be classified as God's gift. Salvation is His gift (Ephesians 2:8-9)—given to those who exercise personal repentance and faith while depraved. Some people would suggest that Romans 12:3 refutes this fact:

> *For through the grace given to me I say to every man among you not to think more highly of himself than he ought to think; but to think so as to have sound judgment, as God has allotted to each a measure of faith.* (Romans 12:3)

The *"faith"* addressed in Romans 12:3 cannot be the faith that God requires prior to effecting salvation. God saves under one condition only: When the depraved repent and choose to believe (Acts 16:31; Acts 26:18; Romans 10:9-19; etc.). We will confirm that God's gift of *"faith"* (Romans 12:3) is the faith needed to function within the area of the New Testament believer's spiritual gifting, a gift received <u>after</u> repenting and believing while depraved.

*F*or sure, the *"faith"* addressed in Ephesians 2:8-9 cannot be classified as God's gift.

According to 1Peter 4:10, Romans 12, 1Corinthians 12 and 14, Ephesians 4, etc., every church saint receives a spiritual gift. This spiritual gift is received in conjunction with being placed into Christ through the avenue of the Holy Spirit (1Corinthians 12:13; Ephesians 1:3) subsequent to exercising repentance and faith while depraved. No doubt, the *"faith"* addressed in Romans 12:3 is of utmost importance if we are to function efficiently within the area of our spiritual gifting. This gift of *"faith"* is <u>not</u> the same *"faith"* as is mentioned in Ephesians 2:8-9. Considering the above, we can conclude the following.

Once we exercised repentance and faith while depraved, we were baptized into Christ's body through the avenue of the Holy Spirit (1Corinthians 12:13) and were *"saved"* (Acts 16:31). In other words, we were *"born again"* (John 3:3-6), became new creations (2Corinthians 5:17), and were made part of the *"body"* of Christ (Ephesians 5:30). In conjunction with being saved, subsequent to exercising repentance and faith while depraved, we received the *"measure"* of *"faith"* mentioned in Romans 12:3, the *"faith"* given to every member of Christ's body, the church, so each gift within His body might function as efficiently and powerfully as possible. This *"faith"* is God's gift (Romans 12:3), unlike the *"faith"* of (Ephesians 2:8-9), which is exercised by the depraved prior to spiritual regeneration.

The *Wycliffe Bible Commentary* records the following regarding Romans 12:3:

> Paul is not here speaking of "saving faith"… "Saving faith" would be no standard for correct self-judgment. Only pride would say: "See how much saving faith I have." But it is a humbling experience to say: "Here is the faith I have for carrying out this or that particular task for God." This can only lead to the prayer, "Lord, increase our faith" (see Luke 17:5). In the account of the heroes of faith in Heb 11, we see that the measure of faith given corresponds to the task to be accomplished. [ii]

Undoubtedly, the *"faith"* of Ephesians 2:8-9, exercised by the depraved in conjunction with recognizing their need for a Savior, must not be confused with God's gift of *"faith"* (Romans 12:3) granted to those who have previously chosen to believe. Yes, God gives believers faith (Romans 12:3), but it is the faith needed to function within the area of their spiritual gifting—not the faith required prior to God's redemptive work of spiritual regeneration. Why can we draw this conclusion? Paul is addressing spiritual gifts in Romans 12. Thus, the *"measure of faith"* of Romans 12:3, given to New Testament believers once they are in Christ, cannot be equated with the *"faith"* of Ephesians 2:8-9—the *"faith"* exercised by the depraved prior to salvation. Those who fail to make this distinction entangle themselves in numerous theological contradictions. After all, why would God plead for the lost (depraved) to exercise faith, all of which will not be saved, if He were the source of such faith, determining from eternity past who will or will not receive it? Such a scenario would make Jesus appear as foolish in passages such as Matthew 23:37:

The "measure of faith" of Romans 12:3, given to New Testament believers once they are in Christ, cannot be equated with the "faith" of Ephesians 2:8-9—the "faith" exercised by the depraved prior to salvation.

> *"O Jerusalem, Jerusalem, who kills the prophets and stones those who are sent*
> *to her! How often I wanted to gather your children together, the way a hen*
> *gathers her chicks under her wings, and you were unwilling.* (Matthew 23:37)

Note that the unbelieving Jews rejected Jesus' offer of salvation due to being *"unwilling."* Their unbelief, therefore, did not result from God failing to provide repentance and faith, as some have incorrectly assumed. (Matthew 23:37 is discussed in much greater depth in the *God's Heart* series distributed by this ministry.)

No doubt, God's *"purpose,"* desire, and will for man can be rejected:

> *But the Pharisees and the lawyers rejected God's purpose for themselves, not*
> *having been baptized by John.* (Luke 7:30)

who desires all men to be saved and to come to the knowledge of the truth.
(1Timothy 2:4)

*The Lord is not slack concerning his promise, as some men count slackness; but
is longsuffering to us-ward, not willing that any should perish, but that all should
come to repentance.* (2Peter 3:9 KJV)

Before moving forward, we must correctly answer the following question: "Is the repentance needed for salvation God's gift, or does it originate with man?" Note Acts 5:31:

*"He is the one whom God exalted to His right hand as a Prince and a Savior, to
grant repentance to Israel, and forgiveness of sins.* (Acts 5:31)

Must God give us faith and repentance <u>before</u> we can repent and believe? Some would answer with a resounding, "Yes!" Does this idea line up with the full counsel of God's Word? After all, *"Peter and the apostles"* (Acts 5:29) stated that both *"repentance"* and *"forgiveness"* have been granted to *"Israel"* (Acts 5:31).

For proper interpretation, we must first understand that the word *"Israel"* in this context points to everyone of Jewish descent, not just Jewish believers. Consider as well that the apostles were speaking to the leaders of the Jews, most of whom had rejected Jesus' Messiahship. Had the apostles been speaking of Jewish believers only, and not the entire Jewish nation, they would have stated this fact in the text. Hence, for *"Israel"* in this context to mean anything other than the entire Jewish nation would have been misleading to their unbelieving Jewish audience. Consequently, those who view the word *"Israel"* as pointing to believers alone are in error.

Here is where our study becomes extremely interesting. First, note that *"repentance"* (Acts 5:31) is <u>granted</u> in the same sense that *"forgiveness"* is <u>granted</u>. Second, if repentance should be God's <u>gift</u>, then the entire Jewish nation has been given *"repentance"* and *"forgiveness."* In that case, every Jew would be saved, which the Scriptures vehemently deny. How then is Acts 5:31 to be viewed? God <u>grants</u> *"repentance"* and *"forgiveness"* to Israel in the sense that He offers all of Jewish descent the <u>opportunity</u> to repent as well as the <u>opportunity</u> to receive forgiveness. The choice is theirs as to whether they, in their depravity, will or will not repent and exercise faith. The same opportunity is made available to both Jews and Gentiles according to passages such as Acts 11:18 and 2Timothy 2:25:

> *G*od <u>grants</u> *"repentance" and
> "forgiveness" to Israel in the
> sense that He offers all of Jewish
> descent the <u>opportunity</u> to repent
> as well as the <u>opportunity</u> to
> receive forgiveness.*

"...then, God has granted to the Gentiles also the repentance that leads to life."
(Acts 11:18)

*with gentleness correcting those who are in opposition, if perhaps God may
grant them repentance leading to the knowledge of the truth,* (2Timothy 2:25)

Conclusion: God grants all Jews and Gentiles the right to exercise personal repentance and faith while depraved. This refutes the false teaching that He must give the gifts of repentance and faith to the spiritually regenerated before they can repent and believe. More information regarding faith and repentance is available in the series titled, *"God's Heart,"* distributed by this ministry. Should you desire more input, just get in touch.

Next week, we will observe the value of suffering. So prepare to be challenged.

Romans 5:1-5 Questions

First Day

1. Read Romans 5:1-5. What is the result of justification (v.1)? How has it changed your life to realize that you *"have peace with God"?* (I am assuming that you are a believer.)

2. Does having *"peace with God"* guarantee that you will always have the peace of God? Explain. How does this tie in with Galatians 5:22-23, 25? What hinders you most from walking in the fruit of the Spirit on a moment-by-moment basis?

3. Did you notice that you attained *"peace with God"* through a Person? Who is this Person? How and why could He provide this *"peace"?* Please don't view this question as too trivial. It is one of the deepest theological issues to cross the mind of man.

Second Day

1. Read Romans 5:1-5. According to Romans 5:2, you have been introduced to (or given *"access"* to—KJV) something as a result of the *"faith"* you exercised while depraved. To what have you been introduced, and how did this *"introduction"* occur? Is Romans 5:2 teaching that you received all the *"grace"* you will need for a lifetime when you were justified? Explain.

2. According to this same verse, what allows the believer to *"stand"* as he experiences the adventure of faith? How does this tie in with 2Corinthians 12:9-10, 1Corinthians 15:10, 2Timothy 2:1, and Hebrews 4:16?

Third Day

1.   Read Romans 5:1-5. If the word *"exult"* (Romans 5:2) means to rejoice, what does the phrase *"exult in hope of the glory of God"* communicate to you? How does this correlate with 2Corinthians 4:16-17? If you are having difficulty answering any of this week's questions, remember that the lesson should assist you.

2.   Did you pray for wisdom as you began answering today's questions? From what is stated in 2Corinthians 4:16-17, how did Paul view *"affliction"*? What is communicated in 2Corinthians 4:18 that explains Paul's steadfastness in the midst of his many trials? Do you view life from this perspective? If not, why not?

Fourth Day

1.   Read Romans 5:1-5. Now that we understand Paul's view of suffering, what does the phrase *"we also exult in our tribulations"* communicate to you (Romans 5:3)?

2.   *"Tribulation"* (suffering) causes a particular character trait to be built into a believer (Romans 5:3). What is this character trait, and how would you define it? Do you possess this trait?

3.   When you experience *"tribulation"* (problems), do you trust God to provide victory; or do you attempt to eliminate your problems in your own strength? What happens when you choose the latter as your temporary way of escape?

Fifth Day

1. Read Romans 5:1-5. Now read Romans 5:4 a second time. After *"tribulation"* has produced *"perseverance,"* what is produced next? When you hear the words *"proven character,"* what thoughts come to mind?

2. Do you know anyone who could be classified as a person who possesses *"proven character"*? What did this person experience, or walk through, that allowed you the privilege of observing his or her *"proven character"*? How would you describe God's character? Is this description based on Biblical truth? If so, what Scriptures?

Sixth Day

1. Read Romans 5:1-5. After *"proven character"* comes *"hope."* In your own words, define *"hope."* What did Paul mean when he stated that *"hope does not disappoint"*? How does this connect with Romans 4:18, Hebrews 6:18-19, and Romans 9:33?

2. Through what means did you receive *"the love of God"* into your heart (Romans 5:5) subsequent to exercising repentance and faith while depraved? What is the difference between what is stated here concerning the Spirit of God and what is stated in Ephesians 5:18 and Galatians 5:22?

Romans 5:1-5 Lesson

Peace with God

Considering last week's study regarding justification, we can understand why Paul used the phrase, *"peace with God"* (Romans 5:1). Not only does God wipe away all sin, but He also builds a peaceful relationship between Himself and those whom He justifies. God is not angry at us. He is at peace with us! In other words, His idea of a good time is <u>not</u> pouncing on us to see how much damage He can inflict. Peace has been restored. We are His children. Yes, He will chasten us when we sin. But, when He does so, He responds in love (read Hebrews 12:4-11). Therefore, when we repent as a believer, we are not restoring our relationship, but our fellowship with the Father. The relationship that was established through justification is an eternal relationship, incapable of being severed by sin.

Possessing *"peace with God"* (Romans 5:1) is quite different from possessing the peace of God. *"Peace with God"* was established for all eternity when He *"justified"* us subsequent to our exercising *"faith"* while depraved. The *"peace"* of God, on the other hand, is a *"fruit of the Spirit"* (Galatians 5:22) and must be received on a moment-by-moment basis. Isaiah was right when he wrote, *"The steadfast of mind Thou wilt keep in perfect peace, because he trusts in Thee"* (Isaiah 26:3). God's *"peace"* is ever present among those who spend more time being a friend to God than a friend to others.

God's "peace" is ever present among those who spend more time being a friend to God than a friend to others.

Notice that *"peace with God"* was made available *"through"* a Person, *"the Lord Jesus Christ"* (Romans 5:1). Yes, Jesus gives every individual the privilege of living in *"peace with"* the Godhead. For this *"peace"* to become a reality, however, repentance and faith must first be exercised by the depraved.

Ample Grace for Trials

We need to know as much as possible about *"grace,"* for through Jesus Christ *"...we have obtained our introduction by faith into this grace in which we stand..."* (v.2). This *"introduction... into...grace"* results in justification and all that this wonderful act includes. Don't think for a moment, however, that this initial measure of grace will sustain us. We need new grace on a daily basis as we trust Christ to keep the trials of life in check.

The great news is that grace is available for any situation we might face. Believers do have, however, the option of either accepting or rejecting this grace. Those who reject it experience defeat, while those who accept it soar like *"eagles"* (Isaiah 40:31). Yes, it is God's grace that causes Him to justify (save) the depraved who repent and believe, but it is also His grace that empowers the believer for service. Paul understood this truth as well as anyone according to 2Corinthians 12:9-10, 2Corinthians 4:7-12, 1Corinthians 15:10, and 2Timothy 2:1.

In Romans 5:2, Paul writes: *"...we exult in hope of the glory of God."* What does he mean by this statement? The answer is simple, especially since the word *"exult"* means "rejoice." Paul is saying that he rejoiced in every hardship, because hardship meant that *"glory"* would follow. He says it well in 2Corinthians 4:17:

> *For momentary, light affliction is producing for us an eternal weight of glory far beyond all comparison,* (2Corinthians 4:17)

No doubt, we can possess hope in the midst of our *"affliction,"* because the *"affliction"* is producing *"an eternal weight of glory"* that will be ours for all eternity. Wow!

Paul exulted (rejoiced) *"in hope of the glory of God"* (Romans 5:2). He also exulted [rejoiced] *"in...tribulations"* (Romans 5:3). In other words, Paul viewed all suffering as his ally; pain had become his friend. How else could he have survived the many hardships described in 2Corinthians 11 and 12? He regarded God as sovereign and working everything *"for good"* (Romans 8:28). That is how he made it. That is how he finished the race!

Most of us do not possess the maturity to view life from Paul's perspective, for we have not yet learned to *"...look...at the things which...are not seen..."* (2Corinthians 4:18). When this is the case, we normally draw our conclusions from that which is visible. In fact, most of us attempt to rectify negative circumstances through our own strength. The Lord, however, allows the same negative circumstances to arise until we have learned to trust God in the midst of our various trials. It is then that we pass the class—be it in the area of finance, a sinful habit, loneliness, a difficult relationship, or whatever. Through an increased understand of God's capabilities, we learn to rest in His provision, sovereignty, and grace, the by-product of which is a perseverance explained only in terms of Christ.

What, then, is perseverance? Perseverance is the ability to remain encouraged when things look thoroughly hopeless. It is the ability to trust our heavenly Father when most are dropping out of the race. Yes, we persevere through accepting His grace for every challenge of life. That is what perseverance looks like, and that is why it is so very necessary to possess.

If we hold fast in *"tribulation,"* allowing God to produce *"perseverance,"* *"proven character"* will result. Isn't it wonderful to hang out with people who have had their character tried and proven? I believe that everyone seeks to know at least one person of that sort, and that God is looking for that person as well (2Chronicles 16:9). As I think of those who possess *"proven character,"* I realize that none of them arrived at that place void of hardship. We all suffer in some form or other, but it certainly is not fun. When we allow our trials to choke and stifle us, they seem virtually unbearable. No matter how difficult they become, however, knowing that God is using them for good encourages us to yield to His grace to see us through. And yes, He will see us through!

We need to take a moment to address God's character, for if we fail to understand Who He is we may hinder the work He desires to accomplish in and through us. In fact, when adversity comes our way, we may attempt to fix the problems ourselves, or worse yet, perceive Him as the cause of it all. The statement: "When we don't understand His hand, we can trust His heart" is so very true. Viewing our trials through the lens of His character is essential for abundant living. The deeper we know Him, therefore, the more we will trust Him in the heat of the battle.

After *"proven character"* comes *"hope"* (v.4). Hope is the ability to look positively at the future regardless of the present circumstances. Those who possess hope in Christ will never, ever be disappointed (v.5). The Object of their hope will see to that.

"...Hope does not disappoint, because the love of God has been poured out within our hearts through the Holy Spirit who was given to us" (v.5). *"The Holy Spirit...was given to us"* at the point of justification, subsequent to our exercising repentance and faith while depraved. It is a one-time shot that never has to be repeated. Consequently, we have access to this *"love"* anytime we need it.

Viewing our trials through the lens of His character is essential for abundant living.

To *"...be filled with the Spirit"* (Ephesians 5:18; Galatians 5:22) is different—it is repeated over and over again in our experiences, occurring only during those times when we walk in fellowship with God. When we are *"filled with the Spirit,"* the love of God—along with His peace, joy, patience, etc.—is manifested to those around us, no matter what has come our way.

God always uses tribulation for our good. It is through knowing His heart, however, that we comprehend the value of this truth. Romans 5:6-11 will supply additional insight into Who God is and what He has done for man.

Romans 5:6-11 Questions

First Day

1. Read Romans 5:1-11. Romans 5:6 states that at some point in time *"we were...helpless."* *"Helpless"* to do what? When and why were we *"helpless"*?

2. Why must man see himself as *"helpless"* before he can experience the salvation provided by God alone? How does this relate to Ephesians 2:8-9, Titus 3:5, Romans 3:20, and similar passages?

3. Verse 6 also states that *"...Christ died for the ungodly."* Do the lost (depraved) have to realize they are *"ungodly"* for God to save them? If so, why is this the case? How does this tie in with what we previously learned regarding repentance?

Second Day

1. Read Romans 5:1-11. Today's question is answered in this week's lesson, but don't go there until you have tackled it on your own. According to Romans 5:6, Jesus died *"at the right time."* To what is Paul making reference? Read the following verses for assistance: 1Corinthians 5:7; Matthew 26:17-18; 27:35; 27:50.

Third Day

1. Read Romans 5:1-11. Now read Romans 5:7 a second time. Is there anyone that you would *"die"* for? List some thoughts that entered your mind as you pondered this question?

2. We find in Romans 5:8 that *"...God demonstrates His own love toward us..."* Where was *"His...love"* demonstrated most vividly? Considering your answer, through what avenue can we best demonstrate God's love?

3. How does the previous question correlate with Matthew 10:39, John 15:12-13, and 2Corinthians 4:11-12?

4. When did you last sacrifice what was rightfully yours for the sake of someone else? What did you learn from that experience? How were you blessed?

Fourth Day

1. Read Romans 5:1-11. Do you realize that God loved us before we loved Him (v.8)? If Jesus *"lives in"* us (Galatians 2:20) and we are *"partakers of the divine nature"* (2 Peter 1:4), why do we sometimes struggle with loving with His kind of love?

2. Find at least five verses that stress the importance of loving God and His people.

Fifth Day

1. Read Romans 5:1-11. Note the phrase, *"...having now been justified by His blood..."* In verse 9. How is it that we could have *"been justified by His* [Jesus'] *blood"?* You may need to review the notes associated with Romans 5:1, a verse that addresses the term *"justified."*

2. What does Paul mean when he writes: *"we shall be saved from the wrath of God through Him"?*

3. God's *"wrath"* will be poured out on man at some point in the future. Who will experience His *"wrath,"* and why will they experience it? How does this relate to Revelation 20:11-15? Note: Materials studied earlier in the course should assist you in answering this question.

Sixth Day

1. Read Romans 5:1-11. Read Romans 5:10 a second time. What does it mean to be *"reconciled to God"?* Through what means is a person *"reconciled"* to Him?

2. Verse 10 also states that *"...having been reconciled, we shall be saved by His life."* What does it mean to be *"saved by His* [Jesus'] *life"* (it is extremely important that we understand this phrase)? From what we studied in association with verse 3, what does it mean to *"exult in God"* (Romans 5:11)?

Romans 5:6-11 Lesson

Helpless to Save Ourselves

Are you ready to digest more meat from the Word?   In Romans 5:6, we see that man is *"helpless"* to save himself. No matter how hard he labors, man can never perform enough good deeds to merit God's favor. Passages such as Ephesians 2:8-9, Titus 3:5, and Romans 3:20 confirm this fact. Many people, however, attempt to gain salvation through their own effort. If man would but realize that he is ungodly, which he is capable of doing while depraved, repent (turn from sin) and exercise faith, God will save him to the utmost.

Have you wondered why so few people choose to repent and come to Christ?   John communicates it best in John 3:19-21, where he states that *"...men loved the darkness rather than the light...,"* as evidenced by the fact that *"...their deeds were evil."* He then states that *"...everyone who does evil hates the light, and does not come to the light, lest his deeds should be exposed."* In other words, a man who enjoys sin will not come to the Lord, for the Lord will expose his error. If man refuses to perceive himself as sinful (ungodly) and, therefore, fails to repent while depraved, he simply cannot become God's child. Paul spent much time proving this truth in Romans 1-3.

Read Romans 5:6 again, paying special attention to the phrase *"...at the right time Christ died for the ungodly."* What a powerful statement for Paul to make at this point in his epistle! Could it be that God appointed a specific time in history, even to the very day and hour, for Jesus to die—all along granting man a free will to choose as he pleases? The answer is "yes." After all, Jesus was crucified at 9:00 A.M. on Passover morning, at the exact time that the Passover Chagigah sacrifice was being offered in the temple. Thus,

> *If man fails to repent while depraved, he simply cannot become God's child.*

He died *"at the right time,"* in fact, the only time that would fulfill the Father's purpose. Note: *The Gospels from a Jewish Perspective* commentary, distributed by this ministry, addresses this subject in great detail. If you should desire to dig deeper, just let us know.

Take a moment to meditate on verses 7-8. As I consider these passages, I can't help but ask myself if I would be willing to die for my brothers and sisters in Christ. Until we are placed in a situation that would require such a decision, I doubt if any of us can know how we would respond. Christ not only died for us, but He did so *"while we were yet sinners."* What love! He actually demonstrated His love through the cross by dying *"for the ungodly"* (Romans 5:6), an act sanctioned by His Father. We can demonstrate this same type of love as we walk by God's Spirit and lose our lives for others (Matthew 10:39; John 15:12-13; 2Corinthians 4:11-12).

Saved from God's Wrath through Christ's Death

Paul continues by saying that because we have *"...been justified by His blood, we shall be saved from the wrath of God through Him"* (v.9). Jesus' *"blood,"* once applied to our lives, allows the Father to justify us (make us not guilty before Him)—since the shedding of *"blood"* is a symbol of the fact that a death has occurred, *"the life of the flesh"* being *"in the blood"* (Leviticus 17:11). At that point, everything we have studied concerning justification applies to us. As a result of being made righteous, holy, blameless, complete, etc., we will escape God's *"wrath."* We will not stand before the *"great white throne"* judgment of Revelation 20:11-15. Only unbelievers will experience that horrible ordeal.

Paul repeats himself quite often, for he realizes the necessity of a deep and abiding understanding of the cross. After all, *"...the cross is to those who are perishing foolishness, but to us who are being saved it is the power of God"* (1Corinthians 1:18).

Saved Daily from Sin's Power by Christ's Life

I don't know of any verse that better communicates the essence of the Christian experience than Romans 5:10. It first states that believers have been *"…reconciled to God through the death of"* Christ, *"reconciled"* meaning "restored to favor." No doubt, God smiled on us at the point of justification, and for the first time we could call Him *"Father"* (Galatians 4:6). We were finally at peace with our Creator. But is this reconciliation all that we received? Did He restore us to a place of favor so we could flounder around until He calls us home? Based on the remainder of the verse, I don't think so.

Most believers understand at least something regarding the first half of Romans 5:10, but few comprehend the awesomeness of the remainder of the verse. In fact, the phrase, *"we shall be saved by His life,"* holds the key to abundant living. Consider the wonderful news that follows.

We understand well by now that at the point of salvation (justification) we, as church saints, were freed from the penalty of sin. But salvation includes more than forgiveness of sins. It includes, among other things, being saved on a day-to-day, moment-by-moment basis from the temptations we face as believers. How is this salvation (deliverance) accomplished? It is accomplished by Jesus' life that moved into our spirit the moment we repented and believed while depraved (Galatians 2:20; Colossians 3:4)! Read it: *"…we shall be saved by His life"* (Romans 5:10). This continual, moment-by-moment salvation is not addressing the issue of getting out of hell and into heaven. The first part of the verse dealt with that topic—salvation from the penalty of sin. Paul is saying that the life of Christ, residing inside us, is the only means through which we experience salvation from Satan's ever-present schemes. Therefore, by yielding to Christ's life within, victorious living becomes a reality rather than remaining an obscure idea understood by God alone.

You may say, "I know (in my head) that I am saved from the penalty of sin, and that temptation is overcome through yielding to Jesus' inward presence, but how does this work in a practical sense?" That is a great question, for we can talk about being saved by Christ's life without knowing much about the subject matter. For this reason, we will spend much of our time in Romans 6, 7, and 8 discussing this vital issue. But for now, let me give you an idea of how this has <u>begun</u> to work in my own experience. Note the emphasis on <u>begun</u>.

I have found, first of all, that temptation cannot be overcome by concentrating on the temptation. If I have a problem with stealing, I will never experience victory in that area by saying, "I cannot steal." With that mind-set, the responsibility of overcoming my problem depends upon me. However, if I see myself as holy and perfect, as God sees me, I will realize that it is unnatural for me to yield to temptation. Consequently, when I am tempted, I can remember that Jesus is living in me, yield to His life, and walk away in His strength. This is what it means to *"be saved by His life"* (Romans 5:10). Sounds simple, doesn't it? But you know as well as I do that it is not as easy as it sounds. Therefore, we will invest significant time in Romans 6:1-8:17 learning how this reality can become more than just a hit or miss exercise of futility. In fact, it must become a consistent way of life if we desire to live victoriously.

> *Temptation cannot be overcome through concentrating on the temptation.*

In Romans 5:11, Paul states that *"…we…exult in God through our Lord Jesus Christ."* From Romans 5:2, we know that *"exult"* means to "rejoice." Rejoice we can, because through Christ we have been reconciled and restored to a place of favor with the Godhead! No wonder Paul described the *"gospel"* as *"…the glorious gospel of the blessed God…"* (1Timothy 1:11)? It truly is *"glorious"*! We will continue to observe just how *"glorious"* it is as we walk through the remainder of this study. Isn't this fun! Next week's material is some of the most thought-provoking input in the entire course, so remain alert.

Romans 5:12-21 Questions

First Day

1. I can hardly wait for you to study this week's material! Read Romans 5:12-21, along with Genesis 2 and 3. Romans 5:12 states that *"through one man"* something *"entered into the world."* Who was the *"man,"* and what *"entered into the world"*? This next question may challenge you, so spend some time thinking through it (if you can't answer it now, you will be able to later). If the word *"sin"* in verse 12 does not refer to an act of sin, to what is it making reference?

2. What was *"spread to all men"* as a result of Adam's disobedience (v.12)? Does the word *"death"* (or dead) in Scripture always refer to physical death? If not, what could it mean? How does this relate to passages such as Ephesians 2:1 and Colossians 2:13?

Second Day

1. Read Romans 5:12-21. The word *"imputed"* means "to charge to a person's account" (v.13). From the time of Adam until the time of the Mosaic Law, *"sin was in the world"* but *"not imputed"* (v.13). What does this communicate to you?

2. How does Romans 2:12 relate to what we have been studying?

Third Day

1. Read Romans 5:12-21. Consider the next question carefully before answering. How could God remain just and allow *"death"* to reign *"from Adam until Moses"* (v.14) if *"sin"* was *"not imputed"* during that time span (v.13)?

2.   Read Romans 5:14 again. How could Adam be *"a type of Him who was to come,"* that is, *"a type of"* Jesus? Be sure to reference both Old and New Testament Scripture while pursuing your answer. Don't become discouraged if you have difficulty completing today's assignment. Just do what you can and be encouraged with your progress! The lesson should help you work through most of your difficulties.

Fourth Day

1.   Read Romans 5:12-21. Paul compares the fruit of Adam's disobedience with the fruit of Christ's obedience in Romans 5:15-19. What does he say regarding Adam and Christ in those verses? What was the most important thing you learned from today's lesson?

Fifth Day

1.   Read Romans 5:12-21. In Romans 5:18, we read that *"...one transgression...resulted* [in] *condemnation to all men..."* How could God condemn all mankind through Adam's sin and, and at the same time, remain just? What did God do that provided an avenue for the repentant sinner to avoid this condemnation?

2.   Does the statement, *"...even so through one act of righteousness there resulted justification of life to all men"* (v.19) teach that all mankind will be saved now that the cross is an actual event in space and time? If not, what does it mean? List some verses that confirm your answer.

Sixth Day

1.   Read Romans 5:12-21. In Romans 5:20, Paul again states the purpose of the Law. What is that purpose? As *"sin increased,"* what else increased? What does this communicate regarding the character of God, especially in the area of grace and mercy?

2.   The word *"eternal"* is used in Romans 5:21. What is *"eternal life"*? If you had difficulty answering this question, the following lesson should assist you.

Romans 5:12-21 Lesson

Adam's Mistake - Jesus' Remedy

In this week's questions, we observed the stark contrast between the awfulness of Adam's disobedience and the greatness of Christ's obedience. Adam's fall brought condemnation to all men, but Christ's sacrifice offered reconciliation to all men. This section also provides a deeper revelation of the word *"sin."*

Before going further in today's lesson, turn to the Reference Section located at the back of your workbook. Nine circle diagrams are provided that will be referenced frequently over the next few weeks. If you want, you can make copies for easy reference. Whatever makes you comfortable is the main issue, for you MUST use them. The written material will be impossible to comprehend otherwise.

The content of the following paragraph may be somewhat confusing at this juncture in the course, but it will become an easy read as we continue to work through this fascinating section of God's Word.

In Romans 5:12, we find, *"...through one man sin entered into the world..."* To properly interpret this phrase, we must take into account that Satan was present in *"the world"* prior to Adam's sin, Satan being the personification of sin. Consequently, the phrase *"...through one man sin entered into the world..."* must mean, *"...through one man sin entered into man..."* Adam was the *"man,"* for God instructed him to abstain from partaking of *"the tree of the knowledge of good and evil"* in Genesis 2:17. Should he partake of it, he would *"die"* instantly in the spiritual sense (Genesis 2:17) and later in the physical sense—it was as simple as that. He ate of the tree in Genesis 3:6 and experienced immediate spiritual death, a death that points to separation rather than extinction. Why separation rather than extinction? *"God is Spirit"* (John 4:24), and Adam's sin separated him from God in the spiritual sense. His physical death came much later, for a son was born to Adam in Genesis 4 after his sinning in Genesis 3, meaning that he remained very much alive physically after his disobedience. Thus, *"sin entered into the world,"* that is, *"entered into"* man, resulting in spiritual separation from God. Note: Genesis 3:7 verifies that this spiritual death did not prevent Adam from recognizing his spiritual nakedness, confirming that the depraved can comprehend their need for a Savior, exercise personal repentance and faith, and experience God's salvation.

Obviously, the word *"sin"* in Romans 5:12, being a noun, can point to something other than man's acts of sin. In fact, it refers to a power called *"sin."* This makes Romans 5:12 intriguing indeed, so enjoy what follows.

To make certain that Romans 5:12 is covered thoroughly, I have divided the passage into phrases and discussed each phrase in as much detail as possible. You will notice that I sometimes repeat myself by saying the same thing in different ways, for you must begin to grasp the principles taught in this verse if the remainder of the course is to be meaningful.

The word "sin" can point to something other than man's acts of sin.

Observe Circle Diagram 1 in the Reference Section titled, *Man is a Three Part Being.* Read all information. When you finish, continue with the lesson.

Therefore, just as through one man sin entered into the world, (Romans 5:12a)

1. The presence of sin was already on earth, but not in man, before Adam sinned. After all, the serpent (evil) was present in the garden before Adam ate of the forbidden fruit. However, when Adam sinned (Genesis 3:6-7), *"sin entered into"* man through *Adam's* disobedience (Romans 5:12). It is obvious that Adam committed an act of sin. But the word *"sin"* in some cases,

especially in portions of Romans 5-8, refers to a power called *"sin"* which entered into Adam and dwells in man. This power is referred to in Scripture as *"the law of sin"* in passages such as Romans 7:23, 25 and 8:2. It is called *"sin"* in verses such as Romans 7:17 and 20. We will refer to this power in most instances as the power of sin, but in some cases simply as sin.

2.   When studying Romans, the context of the word *"sin"* is critical, for it can refer to two totally different things: (1) An act of sin or (2) The power of sin. The power of sin will be discussed on numerous occasions over the next few weeks. You have ample time, therefore, to comprehend its meaning, even if initially it should seem somewhat confusing.

3.   The power of sin *"entered"* into Adam's spirit, soul, and body when Adam disobeyed. As a result, Adam's soul was inundated with messages from this power called *"sin."* Refer to Circle Diagram 2 titled, *Sin (the Power of Sin) Entered into Man,* located in the Reference Section, and read all information. The power of sin is not a demon. It is an organized power that has Satan as its master. If it will help, the power of sin can be

The power of sin is not a demon. It is an organized power that has Satan as its master.

viewed as the opposite of the Holy Spirit. When God speaks to the soul of man, He speaks through the avenue of the Holy Spirit. When Satan speaks to the soul of man, he speaks through the avenue of the power of sin. Thus, the power of sin is Satan's messenger, or agent. We will study this subject in more detail as the course progresses.

and death through sin,

1.   Adam's act of disobedience brought *"death,"* for the Lord had warned Adam in Genesis 2:17 that he would die if he ate of the forbidden fruit. We must remember, however, that the word *"death"* in Scripture can mean "separation" as well as "extinction."

2.   When Adam sinned, his spirit and soul died (they were "separated" from God), at which time the sin nature (Adamic nature, or old man, or old self, etc.) was born. Instantly, it was natural for Adam to sin, because his very nature was sinful, his nature being both soul and spirit. Refer to Circle Diagram 3 titled *Man without Christ,* and notice that the terms dead spirit, sin nature, Adamic nature, old man, and old self are synonymous—expressions that consist of different words but possess the same meaning. When you see one of these terms, either in the course or in Scripture, know that it refers to the nature that Adam possessed after he sinned—the same nature that you and I possessed until we were made new in Christ. Circle Diagram 9 should be referenced as well. We will study Circle Diagrams 1 through 3, along with Circle Diagram 9, in greater detail next week.

3.   The sin nature (or old man, dead spirit, old self, Adamic nature) enjoys rebelling against God. This does not mean that the depraved (the spiritually unregenerated) are incapable of exercising repentance and faith prior to salvation, as was verified earlier.

4.   Because the nature of man is who man is, Adam was the sin nature (the old man, etc.) after he sinned. For more input, refer to Circle Diagrams 1 and 9 and read about the spirit and soul of man.

5.   As was mentioned above, *"death"* in Scripture can mean separation. Because *"God is spirit"* (John 4:24), and since the part of Adam that could communicate with God was separated from God subsequent to his disobedience, Adam was dead to God. Thus, when a man's spirit and

soul are separated from God, the man is dead, even if he continues to live physically. Obviously, the word *"death"* in Scripture does not always point to physical extinction. It can also point to spiritual separation.

6.   When Adam sinned, his spirit and soul died (were separated from God). After all, the power of sin entered Adam's spirit and soul—thereby bringing to life the sin nature (old man, old self, Adamic nature, dead spirit). The power of sin also moved into Adam's body. Adam's soul was then inundated with the power of sin's lies. Refer to Circle Diagrams 2 and 3.

7.   Adam's act of disobedience resulted not only in the immediate death of his spirit and soul, but his physical body eventually died as well. We know that Adam died a physical death several years after he sinned, an event that would not have occurred had he obeyed.

so death spread to all men,

1.   Because we are descendants of Adam, we are born with the nature that Adam possessed after he sinned. Consequently, we are born with a dead (separated from God) soul and spirit because *"death spread to all men."*

2.   Physical death also spread to all men, for Adam eventually died physically, as do his descendants.

because all sinned.

1.   To understand this phrase, we must tie it in with what is previously stated. *"And so death spread to all men, because all sinned"* simply means that our acts of sin confirm that spiritual death spread to all men.

Have you noticed the selfishness of a baby? Cute as they are, babies possess Adam's nature from conception, and as a result, are concerned with one thing only: Getting their needs met. Adults who do not know Christ also exhibit selfish tendencies. Why so? They have the nature of Adam—a nature that is out of touch with God so long as rebellion is chosen over submission to Christ. This nature is determined to have its way, thinking of self above all else. Wasn't this Adam's problem in the garden?

2.   Do you realize that the lost will not be condemned to hell because of their acts of sin? It is the nature they inherited from Adam that will condemn them (Ephesians 2:3—*"...were by nature children of wrath..."*). We will study more about this nature, and what happens to it once a person receives Christ, later in the course.

> *The lost will not be condemned to hell because of their acts of sin.*

3.   Review all of what has been stated regarding Romans 5:12. Refer to Circle Diagrams 1 through 3, and 9, as you do so.

Now that we have covered Romans 5:12, it is time to move on to Romans 5:13. The first part of the verse teaches: *"for until the Law* [the Mosaic Law] *sin was in the world...."* This is obvious, for man has been committing acts of sin since Adam disobeyed in the Garden. Do you realize, however, that these acts of sin are *"not imputed* [charged to a person's account] *when there is no law"*? Man has to break a direct command of God for sin to be counted against him.

But no direct command of God was stated from Adam until Moses, since only the moral law written on man's conscience existed during that time span. Why then did men die from the time of Adam until the time of Moses if they were not in violation of any specific law? The answer is simple. The whole race sinned when Adam sinned. How so? The genes of all of Adam's descendants were in his gene pool when he sinned. Therefore, from God's perspective, all mankind broke His command simultaneously with Adam. This explains why God could remain just and, at the same time, allow individuals to die who lived prior to the issuing of the Mosaic Law. Review Romans 2:12 and observe how it validates our present discussion. Note: Paul is not insinuating that we existed at the time of Adam's disobedience, but rather that our genes were in Adam's gene pool when Adam sinned. In other words, we did not become a person until conception.

Romans 5:14 is easily interpreted with the previous input in mind:

> *Nevertheless death reigned from Adam until Moses, even over those who had not sinned in the likeness of the offense of Adam, who is a type of Him who was to come.* (Romans 5:14)

Do you better understand why our relationship with Adam caused us to need a Savior?

You also read in Romans 5:14 that Adam *"...is a type of Him who was to come"*—*"a type"* of Christ. After all, neither Adam nor Christ has an earthly father. Adam was created void of a sin nature; Christ has never possessed a sin nature. Adam's wife was taken from his side (Genesis 2:21-25); Christ's wife (the church) was taken from His pierced side (John 19:34). Paul's point is quite obvious.

In Romans 5:15-19, Paul verifies that Christ's gift through grace was much greater than Adam's transgression. I once heard it explained this way: "Which would be the greater act, to strike a match and ignite a forest fire, or to extinguish the fire after it was raging out of control?" To extinguish the fire, of course, would be the greater act! No doubt, *"death reigned through the one,"* but *"those who receive the abundance of grace and of the gift of righteousness will reign in life through the One, Jesus Christ."* What incredible news! We can actually *"reign in life"* through yielding to Christ's indwelling presence, which means that we can live above anything that comes our way. Thus, once we exercised personal repentance and faith while depraved and God made us new, He introduced us to the most amazing adventure imaginable—an adventure lived by the life of Another, the life of Christ!

The first phrase of Romans 5:18 states: *"...through one transgression there resulted condemnation to all men...."* As was confirmed earlier on, our genes were in Adam's gene pool when he sinned. Therefore, we were born in a condition that gave God no alternative but to condemn us. We were born with a dead spirit, a spirit separated from God. This separated spirit (commonly called the Adamic nature, old man, old self, dead spirit, or sin nature) made us *"children of wrath"* before the Father so long as we rejected His provision through Christ (Ephesians 2:3).

The believer can "reign in life" through yielding to Christ's indwelling presence.

The last phrase of Romans 5:18 can be misleading if viewed only at surface level. It is <u>not</u> saying that *"through one act of righteousness"* (referring to the cross of Christ) that *"all"* descendants of Adam are saved. Rather, Paul is communicating that through the cross *"justification of life"* (salvation) was made available *"to all men."* No doubt, God requires *"repentance"* (2Timothy 2:25; Acts 11:18) and *"faith"* (Acts 16:31; Acts 26:18; Romans 10:9-10) from the depraved prior to granting such *"life."*

In Romans 5:20, Paul again states the purpose of the Law. The *"Law"* was given *"that the transgression might increase."* Have you, at any time previous to this moment, viewed the Law from this vantage point? Have you ever considered that the Law was given to be broken; that its purpose is to actually make man sin to a greater degree? It was given so man could recognize his sinful state, repent, and receive Jesus as Savior. Notice what happened, however, when the *"transgression"* increased! God's *"grace"* increased as well! Consequently, when man's sin increased, God's grace increased accordingly, giving man ample time to repent and come to Christ should he so desire. Yes, *"sin reigned in death,"* but *"grace"* would *"reign through righteousness to eternal life through Jesus Christ our Lord"* (Romans 5:21).

"Eternal life" (v.21) is God's kind of life. It has no beginning and no end. It is the kind of *"life"* that every New Testament believer receives when placed in Christ. Remember this!

You may be wondering how to incorporate this truth into your everyday experiences. Don't worry, for Romans 6 does a great job of bringing out the practical side of what we have been studying. We start looking at that chapter next week, so be encouraged.

Romans 6:1-6 (Part 1) Questions

Don't forget to pray each day before answering your questions.

First Day

1. Read Romans 6:1-6, and follow by looking over Circle Diagrams 1, 2, 3, and 4 in the Reference Section. Remember that Circle Diagram 3 represents the condition of man <u>without</u> Christ, whereas Circle Diagram 4 represents the condition of man <u>with</u> Christ. Look up all Scripture references, attempting to understand how they tie in with the present subject matter. I highly recommend that you review the section of last week's lesson relating to Romans 5:12. In the space provided below, write down any new insights.

Second Day

1. Read Romans 6:1-6. Man consists of three parts (1 Thessalonians 5:23). From Circle Diagram 1, what are the three parts? What three parts make up the soul? We will study the soul in detail later.

2. What part of Adam died the instant he sinned (take advantage of what we discussed last week)? The nature that Adam possessed <u>after</u> he sinned is referred to in five different ways in Circle Diagram 3. List all five.

Third Day

1. Read Romans 6:1-6. Referring to Circle Diagrams 2 and 3, what entered into Adam's spirit, soul, and body when he sinned? (Feel free to reference last week's notes.)

2. You may be growing weary of answering questions relating to the word *"sin."* Before long, however, you will thank the Lord for having had opportunity to study it in such detail. Write down anything new that the Lord is showing you regarding this three-letter word. Also, make sure to understand what was stated about *"sin"* in last week's lesson. From my own experience, I realize how much review is required before we can get our hands around this enormously important truth.

Fourth Day

1. Read Romans 6:1-6. Circle Diagram 4 (*Man with Christ*) represents a person who knows Christ. From what we studied in Week 7 (Romans 5:1), list a few characteristics of the new man (new self). Note: The new man consists of the spirit and soul of the New Testament believer.

When God says your new man is holy, perfect, blameless, etc., He is saying that your spirit and soul are holy, perfect, blameless, etc. To prove this point, I need only quote Hebrews 10:14 from the New International Version:

> *"because by one sacrifice he has made perfect forever those who are being made holy."* (Hebrews 10:14)

Think about what the writer of Hebrews is communicating here! God makes your spirit and soul *"perfect"* before your behavior has been perfected and made holy (before your behavior lines up with who you are in your spirit and soul). Consequently, what you do is not who you are, even though who you are has a tremendous impact on what you do. Therefore, you are not on a performance based acceptance with God; you are on a Jesus based acceptance with God. Ponder this truth for a few minutes and write down any comments below. If you are having difficulty grasping these truths, don't be discouraged. We will spend much time in the days ahead shoring up our understanding of this subject matter.

Fifth Day

1. Read Romans 6:1-6. According to Circle Diagram 4, where does Christ reside in a New Testament believer? How do Colossians 1:27 and Colossians 3:4 tie in here? Note: Even though Christ and the new man dwell together, the new man and Christ are two distinct entities. We are not teaching that you (the new man) are a little Jesus!

2.   According to Circle Diagram 4, what happens to the power of sin when Christ enters a New Testament believer's spirit? How does 1John 4:4 relate to this truth? Note that the power of sin dwells in the New Testament believer's body only, not in the body, soul, and spirit, as is the case with the lost. In Romans 7, we will study more about this important characteristic of the power of sin.

Sixth Day

1.   Read Romans 6:1-6. What happens to the *"old self"* (old man) when a person finds Christ? (Reference Circle Diagram 4 for assistance.) Now, once again, what is the *"old self,"* and how did he come into existence? (You may need to review last week's lesson to answer properly.)

2.   What does Romans 6:6 teach regarding the *"old self"*? It is extremely important that you answer this next question correctly. Did the *"old self"* (old man) actually die and become extinct when we were made new in Christ, or was it only pronounced dead? If you are having difficulty answering this question, the following lesson should assist your understanding.

Romans 6:1-6 (Part 1) Lesson

The Eradication of the Old Self

This week you have focused on the circle diagram, a tool that should enhance your understanding of Romans 6-8. It is not a flawless tool, but I think you will appreciate its value as we proceed. Much of what is stated in this week's lesson may seem repetitious, but I have learned the necessity of review during the thirty plus years of teaching these materials.

Man consists of three parts: *"spirit...soul, and body"* (1 Thessalonians 5:23). The soul consists of three parts: mind, emotions, and will. We will study the soul in more detail later. Take a few minutes to review Circle Diagram 1.

Circle Diagrams 2 and 3 portray visually what occurred in Adam when Adam sinned. Adam's sin resulted in spiritual death and, thus, a change of nature. This nature is referred to in the Scriptures in several ways: Adamic nature, dead spirit, old self, sin nature, and old man. Therefore, subsequent to Adam's sin, it was natural for Adam to commit acts of sin. Because we are descendants of Adam, we are born in this same condition— *"dead"* to God (Ephesians 2:1), or separated from God, as well as possessors of a nature that enjoys sin.

Not only did Adam's spirit die (it was separated from God, Who *"is Spirit"*—John 4:24), but the power of sin (Satan's messenger, representative, or agent) moved into Adam's spirit, soul, and body (note Circle Diagram 2). Adam's mind, being part of his soul, was then inundated with lies from this power. A review of the lesson associated with Week 10 might be beneficial at this time.

The news is not all bad, however. Man can be freed from the Adamic nature and united with the life of God through Christ. In Circle Diagram 4, we observed that when we exercised repentance and faith while depraved, God *"crucified"* (Romans 6:6) *"our old self"* (Romans 6:6), who we used to be, and created the new self (2Corinthians 5:17), who we are now. This resulted from Jesus taking up residence in our spirit (Colossians 1:27 and Colossians 3:4), along with the Holy Spirit (John 3:5-6; Romans 8:16), which allowed us to be made alive to God. Realize that all of these changes took place at the point of justification (salvation).

God did not clean up our *"old self"*; He *"crucified"* it (Romans 6:6)—eradicated it—did away with it forever. He then created the new self (the new man), which is a holy and perfect being, totally accepted in His eyes.

> *God did not clean up our "old self"; He "crucified" it — eradicated it — did away with it forever.*

For more input regarding the new self (the new man), review the lesson associated with Romans 5:1, realizing that what is stated about justification applies to the spirit and soul of the New Testament believer. No doubt, your spirit and soul define who you are. Thus, the new man is both soul and spirit (reference Circle Diagrams 4 and 9).

If you remember, we discussed Hebrews 10:14 in the fourth day of this week's questions:

> *because by one sacrifice he has made perfect forever those who are being made holy.* (Hebrews 10:14 NIV)

We discovered that God makes our spirit and soul perfect at the point of justification, even though our behavior is being made holy on an ongoing basis. Obviously, what we do is not who we are, even though who we are has a tremendous impact on what we do.

It is important to grasp what took place

> *What we do is not who we are, even though who we are has a tremendous impact on what we do.*

when our *"old self"* (Adamic nature) was eradicated and our new man (new self) was created. The following example, ridiculous as it may seem, has served as a wonderful tool through which to communicate this life changing truth.

If you took a hog (pig), removed its nature and replaced it with the nature of a cat, the resulting creature would use a litter pan. It would have the physical appearance of a hog, but would possess the nature of a cat. So, what would you call the resulting creature? Would you call it a hog or a cat? You would call it a cat, because the nature of a creature, not the way it looks on the outside, makes it what it is. If the resulting creature, the cat, fell into a mud hole, it would lick itself clean. Why? It would lick itself clean because it would hate mud! Cats hate mud; hogs love mud. It is the same with New Testament believers. God, first of all, removed our old nature (*"old self,"* sinful nature, Adamic nature, etc.), for our old nature is who we used to be. He then replaced it with our new nature (the new man, or new self), who we are now. We hate sin, but will, on occasion, commit acts of sin. However, when we do so, we *"…grieve the Holy Spirit of God…"* (Ephesians 4:30), which results in a desire to confess and repent. The bottom line is that we are no longer capable of enjoying sin.

If you took a hog (pig), removed its nature and replaced it with the nature of a cat, the resulting creature would use a litter pan.

Let's expand this cat and hog illustration. As was mentioned earlier in the study, some view the old self (Adamic nature) as wounded, yet alive, in the New Testament believer. In fact, they view the old self (Adamic nature) as eradicated not when we believe, but when we experience physical death. Such a mindset is known as Positional Truth within theological circles, a subject addressed briefly in the lesson associated with Romans 5:1. Is Positional Truth valid, or is it contradictory in nature? It is contradictory, as the following verifies.

Should the old self (Adamic nature) dwell in us, we would possess two natures, making us part evil and part righteous—the old self being evil, the new self being righteous. Thus, we would be both cat and hog, a "cahog." Being part evil and part righteous would present an impossible situation for the New Testament believer. Why so? Should we sin (fall in a mud hole), the hog would be in bliss while the cat would be overcome with grief. On the other hand, should we walk in righteousness (avoid the mud hole), the cat would be in bliss while the hog would be extremely dismayed. Do you see my point? Should we, as New Testament believers, possess two natures, we could never experience God's peace. Either the cat or the hog would be out of sorts no matter what choice was made, leaving our souls in a state of constant disarray! Consequently, either the *"old self"* (Romans 6:6) was eradicated when we were born again or we have no hope of living in God's *"rest"* (Hebrews 4:9) and *"peace"* (Galatians 5:22). The necessity of

Should we, as New Testament believers, possess two natures, we could never experience God's peace.

the *"old self"* (Romans 6:6) being eradicated in the New Testament believer will be validated even more so when Romans 7:1-4 is addressed later in the course.

Now that we have dealt with the eradication of the sin nature in the New Testament believer, let's take a closer look at the power of sin. This power, dwelling in the spirit, soul, and body of unbelievers, bombards their minds with lies on an ongoing basis (Circle Diagrams 2 and 3). The power of sin <u>sends</u> messages to the mind of a New Testament believer, however, through the avenue of the body only, using the believer's brain, a piece of flesh, as the conduit through which to do its work (Circle Diagram 6). Thus, once you are born again (justified), your body is the only avenue through which the power of sin can send a message to your mind.

Don't misunderstand; the body is not evil. It is, however, the avenue through which the power of sin operates as it attempts to control your life. Sin (the power of sin) cannot send messages to your mind through the avenue of the spirit, for in association with Christ entering your spirit the power of sin was evicted (Colossians 3:4; 1John 4:4). Neither can the power of sin enter your soul for the purpose of placing thoughts in your mind, the mind being part of the soul (refer to the circle diagrams). Therefore, when the power of sin sends a message to your mind, it is the thought, and not sin itself (the power of sin), that enters. In other words, the power of sin cannot enter the mind of a New Testament believer.

Take seriously what we are discussing here, for it will serve you well the remainder of your days. If you are having difficulty following, be encouraged. We will invest much time over the next few weeks pursuing these subjects from a Biblical basis. Make sure that Circle Diagrams 1-4 become very familiar. We will use them every day of our lives, especially when confronted with spiritual warfare. We are equipping ourselves for battle, so be sure to remain alert!

I highly recommend Dr. Bill Gillham's work, *Lifetime Guarantee*. It covers several of the truths addressed in Romans 5-8 and has been a source of encouragement to many.

Romans 6:1-6 (Part 2) Questions

Remember to pray for wisdom as you seek answers to this week's questions.

First Day

1. Read Romans 6:1-6. Why would Paul ask the two questions that make up Romans 6:1? How would you answer these questions?

2. Based on Romans 6:2, how did Paul view *"sin"*?

3. Why did some individuals (in Romans 6:1) accuse Paul of teaching license—that a person can receive Christ and bask in sin, love every minute of it, and still view themselves as children of God?

Second Day

Today's questions will challenge you, so ponder them carefully and answer what you can.

1. Read Romans 6:1-6. Romans 6:3 states that New Testament believers are *"baptized into Christ Jesus."* According to 1 Corinthians 12:13, through what avenue were we *"baptized into Christ"?*

2. What does it mean to be *"baptized into His death"* (v.3)?

3. How could we have been *"baptized into His death"* (Christ's *"death"*) when we weren't even alive at the time of *"His death"?* (I warned you that today's questions would be a challenge.)

Third Day

1.   Read Romans 6:1-6. In Romans 6:4, you see the word *"baptism."* Does this word always refer to water baptism? If not, what type of baptism is Paul addressing?

2.   To settle your mind, it might be helpful to do a word study on *"baptism."* (A word study is simply finding out as much about a particular word as possible.) Write down your findings.

3.   What does it mean to *"walk in newness of life"* (v.4)?

Fourth Day

1.   Read Romans 6:1-6. According to Romans 6:6, what happened to the *"old self"* when we were justified (saved)?

2.   What is the *"old self"*? Where did it come from, and why was it alive in you when you were born? (A proper answer may require a review.)

3.   Was the *"old self"* completely *"done away with"* (eradicated) when we received Christ, or was it only pronounced dead? What do Ephesians 4:22-24 and Colossians 3:9-10 say about the *"old self"*?

Fifth Day

1. Read Romans 6:1-6. The words *"body of sin"* in Romans 6:6 actually mean *power of sin* according to *Vine's Expository Dictionary of New Testament Words.* This verse also says that the *"body of sin"* (power of sin) was *"done away with."* If the words *"done away with"* mean *"made powerless,"* what is Paul communicating here? Take your time and do your research. This week's lesson will assist you should you have difficulty answering today's questions.

Sixth Day

1. Read Romans 6:1-6. According to the last phrase of verse 6, what resulted when the *"old self was crucified"* and the *"body of sin"* (power of sin) was *"done away with"* (made powerless)?

2. If you are a believer, had you realized previously that you are no longer a slave to the power of sin? How has learning (or reviewing) that sin has no power over you, encouraged you?

Romans 6:1-6 (Part 2) Lesson

Verses 1-6 of Romans 6 are some of the most fascinating verses in this entire epistle. Why are they so remarkable? They display a side of the cross that can revolutionize every aspect of our walk with Christ.

Paul's Gospel Challenged

Evidently, Paul's enemies had accused him of proclaiming a gospel that granted license (Romans 6:1). Earlier in the course, we learned that license carries with it the idea that believers can live in habitual sin, enjoy sin, and continue to receive God's blessings. Paul's enemies probably said, "Paul, if what you are teaching regarding justification is true, a person can accept Christ, wallow in sin, enjoy every second of it, and rest assured that God is pleased with it all." We know, however, that such thinking is contrary to Paul's teaching. In Romans 6:2, Paul makes the strongest statement possible when he says, *"May it never be."* He then goes on to say, *"How shall we who died to sin still live in it?"* In other words, it is impossible to know Christ and enjoy a lifestyle of habitual sin. Yes, we will sin at times. But repentance and confession will soon follow. Paul's teaching left no room for half-hearted commitments.

It is impossible to know Christ and enjoy a lifestyle of habitual sin.

The Awesomeness of Scriptural Baptism

Romans 6:3 is one of the most misunderstood verses in all of Romans. This verse says:

Or do you not know that all of us who have been baptized into Christ Jesus have been baptized into His death? (Romans 6:3)

We must be careful with the word *"baptized,"* for it does not always refer to water baptism. In fact, when we see the word *"baptized,"* or baptism, etc., water should not automatically come to mind. For example, *"baptism"* in Luke 12:50 refers to Jesus' crucifixion, not to His water baptism of Luke 3:21-22. Thus, words such as *"baptized"* can have different meanings, depending on the context.

This input creates a more than interesting situation in Romans 6:3. Is water the means through which New Testament believers are *"baptized into Christ"*? Not according to 1Corinthians 12:13:

…by one Spirit we were all baptized into one body… (1Corinthians 12:13)

The *"body"* mentioned here is Christ's *"body,"* so think about what this means! It means that the phrase, *"baptized into Christ Jesus"* (Romans 6:3), refers to *"Spirit"* baptism. This is a baptism that occurs in association with justification—a baptism which places a repentant sinner seeking salvation *"into Christ"* so he can be made new. Water can't accomplish such a feat!

Based on this evidence, some might ask, "What, then, is the purpose of water baptism?" The answer is easily obtained, for when we are baptized in water, we are

Water baptism is a symbolic act, a picture of what the Spirit has already done in the realm of the invisible. Thus, water baptism does not save.

saying to the world that we have died with Christ, that we have been buried with Christ, and that we have been raised with Christ to new life—all through the avenue of the Spirit. In other words, water baptism is a symbolic act, a picture of what the Spirit has already done in the realm of the invisible. Thus, water baptism does not save. God saves through placing us in Christ through the avenue of His Spirit subsequent to our repenting and believing while depraved.

What, then, does it mean to *"…have been baptized into His death"* (Romans 6:3)? It means to be identified with His death. This truth is displayed vividly in 1Corinthians 10:2:

> *and all were baptized into Moses in the cloud and in the sea;* (1Corinthians 10:2)

The nation of Israel, while coming out of Egypt, was *"baptized into Moses,"* meaning that they were identified with Moses their leader. Can you see how the word *"baptized"* in this case can mean identification rather than the act of water baptism? Some might ask, "If we were not alive at the time of Christ's death, how could we *"have been baptized into His death"* (Romans 6:3)—identified with *"His death"?* The following diagram provides the answer.

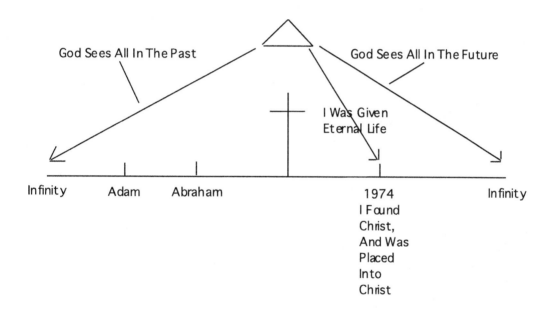

When we were *"baptized"* into Christ through the power of the Holy Spirit (1Corinthians 12:13), we simultaneously received eternal life. As you know, eternal life has no beginning and no end. Consequently, when the Holy Spirit *"baptized"* us into Christ and we received eternal life, the Father saw us as having always been in Christ. He will continue to view us in this manner throughout eternity. Did you comprehend that? Just in case you did not, let me repeat myself. When the Holy Spirit *"baptized"* us into Christ and we received eternal life, the Father saw us as having always been in Christ. Not only this, but He will continue to view us this way throughout

When the Holy Spirit "baptized" us into Christ and we received eternal life, the Father saw us as having always been in Christ.

eternity! Believe it or not, the way God sees us is reality. This explains how we could have been in Christ when He was nailed to the cross, when He was buried, and when He was resurrected. All of this wonderful transformation came about as a result of receiving His kind of life, eternal life, at the point of justification. Remember this truth as we continue.

In Romans 6:4, Paul writes that *"...we have been buried with Him* [Christ] *through baptism into death..."* To comprehend the meaning of Paul's statement, we need only consider what we discussed in the preceding paragraphs. The phrase, *"buried with Him through baptism into death,"* simply means that we have been identified with Christ's *"death."* Because we have been placed (baptized) into Christ through the avenue of the Spirit and are perceived by the Father as having always been in Christ, our death, burial, and resurrection with Christ are a reality. As a result, we can *"walk in newness of life,"* Christ's resurrected *"life,"* a life lived from God's perspective and by His power (v.4).

We now understand how we could have been with Christ when He died (v.3), when He was *"buried"* (v.4), and when He was resurrected (v.4). In fact, Ephesians 2:4-6 states:

> *...God...made us alive together with Christ...and raised us up with Him, and*
> *seated us with Him in the heavenly places, in Christ Jesus,* (Ephesians 2:4-6)

Note the tense used in Ephesians 2:4-6, for it is the past tense. Also, don't overlook the fact that all of these changes occurred as a result of our being placed *"in Christ Jesus."*

Romans 6:5 should now come alive. It states that *"...we have become united with Him* [with Christ] *in the likeness of His death..."* Paul doesn't stop here. He continues by writing: *"...we shall be also in the likeness of His resurrection."* Yes, at some point in the future we will receive a glorified body. But, could Paul also be saying that we can live in Christ's resurrected power in the here and now? That is exactly what he is communicating!

The Old Self Crucified

It is time to address the climax of our lesson. In Romans 6:6, we observe *"that our old self,"* which was inherited from Adam, *"was crucified with Him* [Christ]." What a tremendous statement! This means that the person we used to be *"was crucified"*! Do you understand that? *"Crucified"*! Also, the verb tenses prove that this act occurred in the past, on the cross, and is thus a completed act. This change could transpire due to the kind of life, eternal life, that we received once we were placed in Christ (we addressed this earlier in the lesson). For this reason, and a host of others, I believe that the *"old self"* was completely eradicated when we received Christ (when we were justified). Refer to Circle Diagram 4.

Some perceive the *"old self"* (Romans 6:6) as being <u>declared</u> dead by God yet alive in the New Testament believer. To state it differently, they view God as somehow pretending that the *"old self"* is dead due to their belief that it is alive, yet wounded. They maintain, therefore, that the *"old self"* (Romans 6:6) is only <u>positionally</u> dead—that it must be dealt with until physical death, at which time it is eradicated. What Paul states here is strong proof that such a situation is impossible. No doubt, the *"old self"* (Romans 6:6) was eradicated at the point of justification (when we received eternal life), since it died on the cross with Christ.

A battle takes place inside every church saint between the new self and the power of sin.

That a battle takes place inside every church saint is undeniable. But who are the participants in the battle? Is the conflict between the old self and the new self, or could it be between the new self and the power of sin? The latter is the correct answer, for two verses besides Romans 6:6

speak of the death and eradication of the *"old self."* Colossians 3:9 clearly states that *"the old self"* has been *"laid aside"* (eradicated):

> *Do not lie to one another, since you laid aside the old self with its evil practices,* (Colossians 3:9)

No cause for argument here. Let's next examine Ephesians 4:22:

> *that, in reference to your former manner of life, you lay aside the old self, which is being corrupted in accordance with the lusts of deceit,* (Ephesians 4:22)

The wording of Ephesians 4:22 seems to indicate (on the surface at least) that we must *"lay aside the old self"* on a moment-by-moment basis. Should this be the case, Ephesians 4:22 would contradict Romans 6:6 and Colossians 3:9. While seeking an answer to the apparent contradiction, I discovered a translation by John Murray that resolves the matter. Murray's translation is:

> "so that *ye have put off*, according to the former manner of life, the old man."

As a result, Murray interpreted Ephesians 4:21-22 as follows:

> "You were taught in Christ with regard to the fact that your old man was laid aside."

Thus, Romans 6:6, Colossians 3:9, and Ephesians 4:22 are in agreement. Paul's words in Galatians 2:20 are in agreement as well, for they place the crucifixion of the old self (old man) in the past, never to be repeated:

> *"I have been crucified with Christ; and it is no longer I who live, but Christ lives in me; and the life which I now live in the flesh I live by faith in the Son of God, who loved me, and delivered Himself up for me.* (Galatians 2:20)

This truth can provide incredible encouragement during times of intense warfare, as we will observe later.

We also read in Romans 6:6:

> *knowing this, that our old self was crucified with Him, that our body of sin might* be *done away with...* (Romans 6:6)

The phrase, *"body of sin,"* is quite interesting. *Vine's Expository Dictionary of New Testament Words* defines it as:

> "a governing principle or power...an organized power, acting through the members of the body." [iii]

It is unnatural, therefore, for us to yield to the power of sin's influence.

Coupling this input with the fact that *"done away with"* actually means "made powerless," or "to be rendered idle," we can conclude that the *"body of sin"* (power of sin) has been "made powerless," or "rendered idle," due to the *"old self"* having been eradicated. How liberating! It is unnatural, therefore, for us to yield to the power of sin's influence. Yes, we will commit acts of sin so long as we live in earthly bodies, but every act of disobedience will be an unnatural event. No wonder the last phrase of Romans 6:6 states, *"…that we should no longer be slaves to sin."* Isn't Romans a great book?!

Romans 6:7 Questions

First Day

1. Read Romans 6:1-7. Be sure to ask the Lord for wisdom. In Romans 6:7, we see the phrase, *"for he who has died is freed from sin."* Yes, we have been freed forever from the domination of the power of sin, a fact that will be verified on numerous occasions as we continue. A slight detour is required, however, to determine if we have been freed from the penalty of sin. It is imperative that we understand the number of sins (acts of sin) that were forgiven at the point of justification. We will take this week to research the subject, so prepare yourself for an exciting journey.

2. Review any verses that might assist you in studying the topic of forgiveness. Write down any comments below.

Second Day

1. How do the following verses relate to the degree to which a New Testament believer is forgiven: Ephesians 4:32; Colossians 2:13; 1 John 2:12; Hebrews 9:26; 9:28; Jude 24?

Third Day

1. How do Hebrews 10:10, 10:12, and 10:14 tie in with what we are studying regarding forgiveness? Where and when did this *"offering"* take place?

2. What would be required of Jesus should forgiveness occur on an ongoing (daily) basis in a New Testament believer's life? In other words, what would Jesus need to do if the sin I commit today is forgiven when I confess it? Think long and hard before recording your answer.

Fourth Day

1. If God forgave your past, present, and future sins at the point of justification (when you were placed in Christ subsequent to repenting and believing while depraved), is it possible for 1John 1:9 to teach that you must ask for forgiveness each time you sin? If not, what is 1John 1:9 communicating regarding forgiveness?

2.   As you consider how to answer the following question, remember that we are to interpret Scripture based on the context in which it is written. Does Matthew 6:12, a portion of the Lord's Prayer, teach that a New Testament believer must, on an ongoing basis, seek <u>forgiveness</u> for the sins committed <u>after</u> being saved? In other words, is Jesus teaching that the sins you commit as a believer are forgiven when you confess them? If not, why not?

Fifth Day

1.   If all past, present, and future sins are forgiven at the point of justification, how should the sins committed after justification be dealt with?

2.   Write out a prayer of confession. How does repentance apply here?

Sixth Day

1.   How does Colossians 2:13-14 relate to our present subject matter?

2.   If we were forgiven for all past, present, and future sins at the point of justification, will we suffer *"consequences"* in this life from the sins committed as believers? Read Colossians 3:25 for assistance, keeping in mind that the book of Colossians was written to believers.

3.   What is the most important truth you have studied this week?

Romans 6:7 Lesson

Forgiveness Complete

I can hardly wait to cover this week's lesson. If what is taught here affects your life the way it has mine, you are in for a treat!

The great news is that we have been released from the power of sin through our death with Christ on the cross:

for he who has died is freed from sin. (Romans 6:7)

The *"old self"* (Adamic nature) has been *"crucified"* (Romans 6:6), and we are free to say "no!" to any thought the power of sin sends into our mind. Paul's message is that no *"crucified"* man can respond to any sort of stimulus. Consequently, because the *"old self,"* who naturally desired to sin, is eradicated, it can no longer respond to the power of sin's lies. The new man, therefore, who naturally desires righteousness, can refuse any thought from the power of sin's arsenal of untruths. Some would ask, "Why then do New Testament believers continue to sin?" The answer is provided in subsequent lessons, but a short detour is mandatory before proceeding.

As was stated above, we are no longer enslaved to the <u>power</u> of sin. After all, our *"old self"* was eradicated on the cross (Romans 6:6-7). But, are we freed from the <u>penalty</u> of sin as well? In other words, how many of our acts of sin were forgiven when we were made new in Christ? Were only our past sins forgiven, or were our future sins also forgiven? We need to forever settle this issue, for a life of victory is unattainable without a thorough knowledge of the depths of God's forgiveness. I will use terminology that may be somewhat foreign as we progress through today's lesson. Just digest what you can and leave the remainder for later. In time, everything will come together.

This week's questions addressed forgiveness; passage such as Ephesians 4:32, Colossians 2:13, Hebrews 9:26, 10:10, 10:14, and 1John 2:12 were referenced. If you have studied Greek, please take time to notice the tenses of the verbs and participles contained in these passages. You will be amazed at how often the aorist and perfect tenses are used. ["Aorist" is a Greek term that in this instance points to past action.] This tells us that forgiveness had to be dealt with in the past, at one particular point in time—at the cross.

Let's draw on what we have learned in previous lessons and relate it to this week's truths. When we accept Christ, we are placed into Christ (1Corinthians 12:13; 2Corinthians 5:17). We receive eternal life, and God sees us as having always been in Christ, and as having always been holy, perfect, complete, blameless, and forgiven. We are a finished product in the eyes of the Father, all of this transformation having occurred at the point of justification. Simple, isn't it?

Forgiveness, then, is <u>not</u> something that must be received on an ongoing basis. Christ would need to be re-crucified each time we sin should forgiveness be granted through our asking for it. Remember that Hebrews 10:10 states:

By this will we have been sanctified through the offering of the body of Jesus Christ once for all. (Hebrews 10:10)

We are not obligated to seek forgiveness for sins committed <u>after</u> salvation.

Christ's body was offered once, never to be offered again. Thus, all forgiveness is complete when Christ's blood is initially applied to our lives. This total clemency is what justification is all about; it allows God the Father to make us holy, blameless, <u>and forgiven</u>. We are not obligated to seek forgiveness for sins committed after salvation. In fact, we live in a state of forgiveness.

Even so, the story is not quite complete. Yes, we are no longer required to ask for forgiveness when we sin, but we <u>are</u> required to confess sin once it is committed. Confession means to speak the same thing about sin that God speaks about sin—calling sin what it is before Him. Repentance is a change of attitude which involves both a turning from sin and a turning to God (2Corinthians 7:9-10). Thus, we are required to <u>confess</u> and repent of sins committed after salvation (justification), not to receive forgiveness, but for the restoration of <u>fellowship</u> with the Father. We are eternal beings who have been eternally forgiven. Why would the Lord require us to ask for something we already have? That situation would be totally unreasonable!

Have you wondered why the Lord requires us to confess and repent when our sins are already forgiven? It is because sin severs our <u>fellowship</u> with God—and God created us for the purpose of fellowship. When we sin, the broken fellowship is our problem—not God's. God took care of His side of the problem on the cross. Consequently, He waits (in His mercy and grace) until we repent and confess, at which time fellowship is restored.

Confession can be beneficial in other ways as well. For example, a young couple asked that I hold them accountable prior to marriage. They wanted to remain pure until the wedding day, so they were concerned enough to do something extremely radical. They suggested that I ask them (on a weekly basis) if they were abiding by the guidelines they had established for their relationship. I agreed to do so, and the outcome was very encouraging. They both said that their relationship grew deeper as a result of their decision, and that their accountability with me was a tremendous motivation to remain pure. Why did that accountability provide incentive? They both realized that compromise would require a face to face confession before the man holding them accountable. Do you see my point? God knows that the accountability of confession stimulates us to say "no!" to temptation. Thus, God uses confession and repentance for our good—to enhance our desire to walk in holiness.

Conclusion: We are to confess and repent of sins for two reasons: (1) To have fellowship restored with the Father (2) To motivate us to walk away from temptation through yielding to Christ's life within (Romans 5:10).

Some maintain that after salvation (justification), we are forgiven for each sin committed when we ask for forgiveness. A verse used to support this position is 1John 1:9, which in actuality reveals nothing regarding <u>when</u> the New Testament believer's sins are forgiven—that is, the sins committed <u>after</u> salvation.

> *If we confess our sins, He is faithful and righteous to forgive us our sins and to cleanse us from all unrighteousness.* (1John 1:9)

The verbs *"forgive"* and *"cleanse"* are in the subjunctive mood, and time cannot be plugged into this mood. The subjunctive mood indicates <u>kind</u> of action, not <u>time</u> of action; so 1John 1:9 <u>cannot</u> teach that New Testament believers are required to seek <u>forgiveness</u> for sins committed subsequent to salvation. If sins had to be forgiven after salvation, church saints who died with unconfessed sin would enter heaven with sins not yet forgiven. Impossible! I don't know about you, but the longer I walk with Christ the more I detect hidden areas of immaturity and disobedience—a condition that will remain until physical death. Thus, the entire forgiveness issue had to be dealt with at the point of justification. How else could God accept us into His family?

If sins had to be forgiven after salvation, church saints who died with unconfessed sin would enter heaven with sins not yet forgiven.

Another verse that <u>seems</u> to indicate that we are to seek forgiveness for sins committed after salvation (justification) is Matthew 6:12. This verse is very familiar because it is included in the Lord's Prayer. Here Jesus said:

> *And forgive us our debts, as we also have forgiven our debtors.* (Matthew 6:12)

On the surface it seems that the Lord is instructing <u>all believers</u> to ask for forgiveness once sin is committed. Before jumping to this conclusion, we must consider a more than pertinent question. Did Jesus make this statement before or after the cross? It is obvious that He made it prior to His crucifixion and that the forgiveness issue had not yet been settled. In fact, we learned earlier in the course that none of the Old Testament sacrifices took away sin (Hebrews 10:4, 11); they only covered sin by serving as atonement for sin. Because Scripture must be interpreted in the context in which it is stated, Matthew 6:12 is no exception. Jesus was addressing individuals who lived prior to the cross, meaning that their forgiveness would occur in the future. It was proper, therefore, for them to seek forgiveness. Things changed after the cross, for we are privileged to have had all sin removed in the past. Please don't hear me saying that the teachings of Jesus are outdated or irrelevant. I am simply trying to communicate that all Scripture must be interpreted in context, even the teachings of Jesus.

To determine <u>when</u> a New Testament believer's sins are forgiven, it is doctrinally sound to consider passages such as 1John 2:12:

> *I am writing to you, little children, because your sins are forgiven you for His name's sake.* (1John 2:12)

When Christ's blood was applied to our lives, at the point of justification, forgiveness was thorough and complete.

Here the word *"forgiven"* is in the indicative mood, a mood which <u>can</u> express time. It is also in the perfect tense, a tense that indicates <u>completed action with a resulting state of being</u>. Ephesians 4:32, Colossians 2:13, Hebrews 9:26, Hebrews 9:28, Hebrews 10:10, Hebrews 10:12, Hebrews 10:14, Jude 24 and other passages also indicate that all sin was dealt with when Jesus died. We can conclude, therefore, that when Christ's blood was applied to our lives, at the point of justification, forgiveness was thorough and complete.

We must remember this wonderful news. In fact, we should renew our minds with this truth on an ongoing basis. The following statements summarize what has been expressed.

1. When we were lost (depraved), we repented and exercised faith. It was then that God saved us by eradicating our *"old self"* and, in turn, forgiving our sin.

2. At the point of salvation (justification), our past, present, and <u>future</u> sins were forgiven. We were also given eternal life and made into eternal beings. As a result, God sees us as having always been in Christ and as having always been forgiven. In fact, we live in a state of forgiveness!! This is what justification means: To be forgiven and made not guilty for all eternity.

3. After we are saved (justified), we continue to confess and repent of sin. We do so, however, realizing that our sin is forgiven <u>prior</u> to bringing it before the Father. We must constantly remember that God forgave all past, present, and <u>future</u> sin at the point of justification, subsequent to our exercising repentance and faith while depraved. Confession and repentance after salvation are for the purpose of restoring <u>fellowship</u> with the Father—not for the purpose of receiving forgiveness.

4.   Having become aware of this wonderful truth, we should be less prone to harbor unconfessed sin. In fact, we should be motivated to rush to the Father the instant we disobey, knowing that He will receive us with open arms (Hebrews 4:14-16).   Isn't it freeing to realize that once we are born again we don't confess sin for the purpose of receiving forgiveness, but that confession restores fellowship instead?

Confession and repentance after salvation are for the purpose of restoring <u>fellowship</u> with the Father—not for the purpose of receiving forgiveness.

Understanding this truth transforms the manner in which life is perceived. In fact, our love for Christ becomes the motivation for service—not duty or law. His heart becomes our treasure, not the temporal which fades away. Our passion to walk in constant fellowship with God will become our motivation for daily living. It is then that the world will see Jesus in and through us and, hopefully, desire to know this wonderful, loving, forgiving God Who is our life.

Thank you, Lord, for your indescribable gift!

Next week's questions and lesson address spiritual warfare, so prepare yourself for an exciting journey.

Romans 6:8-11 Questions and Lesson

First Day

1.   Read Romans 6:1-11. Romans 6:8 states that *"...we...died with Christ..."*—remember that it was our old self (Adamic nature, old man, dead spirit, or sin nature) that died with Him. Take what we have recently discussed and describe how we could have *"died with Christ."*

2.   Verse 8 also states that *"...we shall also live with Him."* What thoughts run through your mind when you consider living with Jesus? How can thinking about our eternal home assist us while facing difficult circumstances?

3.   We dealt with this issue earlier in the course, but it won't hurt to refresh our memory. Christ was *"raised from the dead"* (v.9). How important is His resurrection to our faith (read 1Corinthians 15:12-19 should you need assistance)? Is it any wonder that God's enemies so desperately attempt to discredit Christ's resurrection?

4.   From verse 9, we understand that Christ will *"never...die again."* How does this confirm that forgiveness is complete when Christ's blood is initially applied to a New Testament believer?

Second Day

1.   Are you remembering to pray for wisdom? Read Romans 6:1-11. In verse 10, we find that Jesus *"died to sin."* As we confirmed earlier, He also died <u>for</u> sin. No doubt, Jesus' blood was the means through which our sins were forgiven. We will confirm later that His <u>body</u> was the means through which our sinful nature was eradicated. You might want to meditate on that thought for a few moments. Something else needs to be considered. When Jesus allowed man to nail Him to the cross, He also died <u>to</u> the power of sin (Satan's agent) that attacked Him while submitting to the Father's will. In fact, all His life He considered Himself dead to the power of sin. Had this not been the case, He would have sinned, and in the process forfeited His right to be Savior. Write down any comments below.

2.   Verse 10 also states that Jesus *"lives to God."* How can the principles taught in Romans 12:1 and Galatians 2:20 encourage us to live in the same manner?

Third Day

1.   Read Romans 6:1-11. Review Circle Diagrams 3 and 4 (*Man without Christ* and *Man with Christ*). This week we will discuss the practical side of how we function by studying Circle Diagram 5, *How We Operate*. We discover there that man is made up of three parts: body, soul, and spirit. The soul includes the mind, emotions, and will; you think with your mind, feel with your emotions, and make choices with your will. You should also note that your brain is part of your body, and that your habit patterns are stored in your brain. These habit patterns are represented by lines drawn through the brain. Some habit patterns are larger (stronger) than others, which explains the differences in their widths. Make sure to understand what is discussed here before moving forward. Write down any comments below.

2.   Using Circle Diagram 5 as a visual aid, we will now address how we operate. Suppose you happen to be fearful of mice. If these ferocious little monsters should petrify you, a habit pattern that can cause you to respond irrationally in their presence will be formed in your brain, which is a piece of flesh (meat). In fact, when your eye spots one of these fierce creatures, the information will travel up the optic nerve to the brain. The brain will then process this data and give input to the mind. At this time, things become extremely interesting! Because the information given to the brain has to do with mice, and because a large, negative habit pattern is stored there pertaining to mice, the information that leaves the brain and enters the mind causes strange things to happen in the remainder of the soul. In fact, when the mind receives this information from the brain, the emotions are automatically aroused. Both the mind and emotions give input to the will. At that point the will chooses to operate the body in high gear and move it as fast as possible from the impending danger. Finally, it is safe! Study this diagram until you understand it fully and record your comments below.

3.   Are you realizing the extent to which you can be controlled by what you see, touch, taste, hear, and smell? Why, then, should you guard your senses from ungodly influence? Can you think of verses that speak of shielding your mind from that which is harmful? Record your thoughts below.

Fourth Day

Observe Circle Diagram 6, *How the Power of Sin is Defeated*. This diagram illustrates how the power of sin (Satan's messenger, or agent) is defeated when you walk in God's Spirit. Paul says that you are to *"consider"* yourself *"dead to sin, but alive to God in Christ Jesus"* (Romans 6:11). No doubt, you are forgiven of your acts of sin and released from the penalty of those sins if you are born again. Now that you live *"in Christ,"* the power of *"sin"* can be overcome as well. In fact, because Jesus overcame sin's power and you now live in Him (2Corinthians 5:17) and He in you (Galatians 2:20), you can also *"consider"* yourself *"to be dead to sin* [dead to the power of sin], *but alive to God in Christ Jesus"* (v.11).

Let's discuss how this situation is experienced in a practical sense. What if, for instance, you struggle with depression, especially on cloudy days? In such cases, a habit pattern will have been formed in your brain relating to this behavioral issue. How do you suppose this habit pattern was formed? It was molded through repeatedly believing the power of sin's lie. Therefore, *"sin"* will use the stimulus (clouds) in an attempt to ruin your day (Circle Diagram 6) by sending messages to your mind such as, "I always feel depressed on cloudy days. I think I will just lie in bed until this feeling subsides," or, "I don't think I can make it through this day." Did you notice the use of the pronoun "I"? Sin's goal is to deceive you into believing that the thought, which is a lie, is the truth. In fact, by sending the message into your mind through the ungodly habit pattern etched in your brain, sin's lie enters your mind sounding like it has been generated by you. Consequently, the voice you hear is identical to your voice, including accent and dialect. This is where Romans 6:11 comes into play. Sin's lie can immediately be replaced with the truth by considering yourself *"dead"* to what you have just heard. You can do so only because the being who consistently bought sin's lie as the truth, the *"old self,"* has been eradicated (Romans 6:6). Yes, because the old self has been replaced with the new self, you, the new self, have been *"freed from* [the power of] *sin"* (Romans 6:7). Reference Circle Diagram 6 and read what is written at the bottom of the page regarding ungodly habits and the power of sin. Note: The power of sin cannot enter your mind now that you are a believer; it is sin's thoughts that enter your mind. It sends messages into your mind through the avenue of the ungodly habit patterns lodged in your brain.

The power of sin's mission is to trick you into responding to its lies. The only way these thoughts (lies) can be overcome is through the truth of God's Word. Matthew 4:3-11 validates this principle, for Jesus processed evil thoughts without committing sin. After all, to respond to Satan as He did, He was required to process Satan's lies—proving that a thought does not become an act of sin until we buy it as the truth and act accordingly.

We can respond to the power of sin in a similar fashion. When evil thoughts bombard our minds, we must appropriate truth immediately. The first thing required is to remember that *"...our old self was crucified..."* (Romans 6:6), for it serves as a reminder that sin is no longer a natural act. Although we will commit acts of sin so long as we dwell in earthly bodies, sin is an unnatural response because of our new nature—remember the cat illustration. Second, we must *"consider"* ourselves *"dead"* to sin's thoughts *"...but alive to God in Christ Jesus"* (Romans 6:11). To respond in this manner we simply say, "I am dead to this lie floating around in my mind, and I take authority over it in the name of Christ." At that point we should yield to the truth sent into our minds by means of the Spirit, truth that relates to our particular situation. This truth, empowered by the Holy Spirit, overrides the evil thought and we are immediately delivered.

As you probably realize, this godly response is much easier to talk about than experience in daily living. We will have ample opportunity to use what we are learning, for God doesn't teach so truth might lie dormant. He is preparing us for spiritual warfare, so remain alert!

Write down any new insights below.

Let's take a moment to discuss the emotions by referencing Circle Diagram 6, *How the Power of Sin is Defeated*. When the power of sin attempts to stimulate depression (by sending negative thoughts into our minds through the ungodly habit patterns in our brains), the emotions respond immediately. We will begin to <u>feel</u> depressed, especially on cloudy days, as indicated by the diagram. The key at such times is to *"consider"* ourselves *"dead"* to these thoughts (Romans 6:11) and *"alive"* to the truth, truth such as Psalm 118:24:

> *This is the day the Lord has made; let us rejoice and be glad in it.* (Psalm 118:24)

Through faith, which is an element of the mind, along with the empowering of the Holy Spirit, we can choose to set our minds on truth. We can also force the will to accept the input from the mind and reject the input from the emotions, even when the emotions are totally out of sync with reality. This means that, as we walk in the Spirit, we will many times be acting one way while feeling another. In other words, if we refuse to allow our emotions to control our behavior, we will frequently find ourselves responding in an obedient manner while feeling depressed. The great news is that the emotions will eventually settle, and the habit patterns that once incapacitated us will become manageable. In fact, the Lord greatly reduces the strength of these negative habit patterns as we mature in our walk with Him. Note: It is wonderful when the emotions line up with reality, but these seasons are normally short in duration and cannot be expected to be the norm.

We must remember that the emotions can't always be trusted, especially during times of intense spiritual warfare. If we choose to walk opposite of how we feel, the power of sin will attempt to convince us that we are nothing more than hypocrites. To stand, we must realize that many times we will respond positively to truth while <u>feeling</u> like doing just the opposite. This emotional battle is what Jesus faced in Luke 22:44. At Gethsemane, His emotions were out of control, even to the point that *"...His sweat became like drops of blood..."* But, He set His mind on truth, told His will to disregard His emotions, and walked to the cross in the Father's strength. Was He a hypocrite by responding in this manner? Of course not, but we can rest assured that the power of sin was telling Him otherwise.

If we can grasp what we are studying here, through the assistance of the Holy Spirit, we will be amazed at the difference it will make in our ability to persevere in God's strength. We will study more about this subject in next week's lesson, so don't be discouraged if understanding is lacking. It will come together very soon.

Fifth Day

Read Romans 6:1-11. Today, you will answer questions for the purpose of review. Try to answer as many of these questions as possible. Have fun, for we are learning to fight spiritual battles with spiritual weapons!

1. Man consists of three parts. List the three parts. List the three parts of the soul?

2. The *"old self"* makes up what part of an unbeliever? What is the *"old self"*? What happens to the *"old self"* once the depraved choose to repent and believe? According to Romans 6:6, where did it die? How can this be?

3.   The new self (new man) makes up what part of a New Testament believer? What is the new self? How does God view the new self.

4.   Where are habits stored? What is the power of sin? Where does the power of sin live in a lost person? Where does it live in a New Testament believer? What does it attempt to activate in the brain?

5.   What thought process should you apply, with the assistance of the Holy Spirit, when evil thoughts enter your mind? Incorporate Romans 6:6 and 6:11 in your answer.

6.   How do your emotions come into play while dealing with the power of sin? If your desire is to walk in a godly manner, how must your mind and will work together when the emotions are out of control?

Sixth Day

1.   Ask the Lord to help you recognize the lies that the power of sin sends into your mind over the next 24 hours. At the end of the 24-hour period, record the different ways the power of sin attempted to deceive you. We will learn more about spiritual warfare next week, so expect to be blessed. You are doing great!

Romans 6:12-23 Questions

First Day

1.   Read Romans 6:12-23. Turn to the Reference Section and examine Circle Diagrams 7 and 8, *Sin in Control* and *Spirit in Control*. Read Romans 6:12-13 to observe how the circle diagrams relate to these verses. As you read, remember that the word *"sin"* in Romans 6:12 refers to the power of sin. Write down any comments below.

2.   What could Paul possibly mean when he writes, *"...do not let sin reign in your mortal body..."* (Romans 6:12)? What have you failed to do when you allow the power of *"sin"* to *"reign in your...body"*? How do you feel subsequent to being deceived by sin's lie?

3.   Describe your thought processes when you sense that *"sin"* is attempting to *"reign in your...body"*

Second Day

1.   Read Romans 6:12-23. Romans 6:13 states that we are to *"present"* ourselves *"to God as those alive from the dead."* Describe how this presentation is done?

2.   How do we *"present"* the *"members"* of our body *"as instruments of righteousness to God"* (Romans 6:13)? The information and terminology provided in Circle Diagram 8 can assist you with your answer.

Third Day

1.   Read Romans 6:12-23. According to Romans 6:14, the power of *"sin"* is no longer *"master over you."* Why is this so?

2. Why does being freed from *"law"* free you from the dominance of the power of *"sin"* (v.14)?

3. What does the power of sin do when exposed to law? How does this truth relate to Romans 5:20?

Fourth Day

1. Read Romans 6:12-23. Why would Paul include the questions addressed in Romans 6:15? How would you respond should someone ask, *"Shall we sin* [commit acts of sin] *because we are not under law but under grace?"*

2. According to verses 15-16, how did Paul answer the questions addressed in the first portion of verse 15? What does this tell you about Paul's view of sin (acts of sin)?

3. Even though we are forgiven, do we still suffer consequences in this life when we commit acts of sin? Be sure to reference Colossians 3:25, 2Peter 2:19, and Romans 6:16 before recording your answer?

Fifth Day

1. Read Romans 6:12-23. No doubt, we *"were slaves of sin"* before we met Christ (v.17); we were in the condition illustrated by Circle Diagram 3. How does this affect your attitude toward the lost?

2. What does the phrase, *"obedient from the heart,"* communicate to you (v.17)?

3. According to Romans 6:18, something resulted when we were *"freed from sin."* What resulted? How does this truth encourage you?

Sixth Day

1. Read Romans 6:12-23. Take Romans 6:19 through Circle Diagrams 3 and 8. Write down any comments below.

2. What results when you *"present your members as slaves to righteousness"* (v.19)?

3. What does *"sanctification"* mean in verse 19? I thought we studied in Week 7 (Romans 5:1) that a New Testament believer is sanctified at the point of justification? What type of sanctification is Paul addressing here? How does this tie in with Hebrews 10:14, which states:

> *"For by one offering He has perfected for all time those who are sanctified* [being sanctified]." (Hebrews 10:14 NASB)

> *"because by one sacrifice he has made perfect forever those who are being made holy"* (Hebrews 10:14 NIV)?

4. Take what we have discussed and record what Romans 6:20 communicates to you.

5. What does Romans 6:21 communicate regarding life without Christ?

6. What does it mean to be *"enslaved to God"* (v.22)? Didn't Paul say something about this enslavement in Romans 1:1? How did he describe himself there? According to Romans 6:23, what is *"the wages of sin"*? What is God's *"gift"* to man, and where is it found (v.23)?

Romans 6:12-23 Lesson

Freed from the Power of Sin

This week we have verified that the New Testament believer is no longer enslaved to the power of sin. Circle Diagrams 7 and 8, *Sin in Control* and *Spirit in Control,* should have been helpful as you worked through this week's questions.

We first discovered that the word *"sin"* in Romans 6:12 refers to the power of sin. We also learned that if we are not careful, we will allow this power to *"reign"* in our *"body."* When this predicament occurs, we have believed the power of sin's lie and responded accordingly. Yes, sin can *"reign"* if we refuse to remain alert (1Peter 5:8). When we allow this situation to transpire, we should immediately confess our sin, set our mind on truth, and walk in the truth that the Spirit supplies. It takes *"good"* to *"overcome evil"* (Romans 12:21), and nothing can *"overcome"* the power of sin but the *"good"* truth of the Word of God empowered by the Holy Spirit.

While under attack, we are to *"present...[ourselves] to God as those alive from the dead"* (Romans 6:13). We do so by first recognizing that we are powerless against the enemy's schemes. After acknowledging this fact, we then yield to the only Source of deliverance, the *"God"* Who lives in us (Romans 6:13). Because we are *"...seated...in the heavenly places, in Christ Jesus"* (Ephesians 2:6), with the *"old self"* (Adamic nature) having been eradicated (Romans 6:6), the power of sin has lost its grip on our lives. Consequently, the physical *"members"* of our *"body"* (hands, feet, eyes, etc.) are free to respond *"as instruments of righteousness"* as we *"present"* ourselves *"to God"* (Romans 6:13), the Omnipotent Creator. This is what it means to be *"saved by"* Christ's *"life"* (Romans 5:10), Jesus being *"God"* (Hebrews 1:8). Truly, what a wonderful adventure awaits those who choose the road less traveled.

Satan desires to control our mind, for it is in the mind that faith dwells. We must, therefore, guard our thoughts; the power of sin does not slumber when left unattended. We are holy and blameless saints. But even so, *"...when lust has conceived, it gives birth to sin..."* (James 1:15), *"sin"* that must be confessed for fellowship to be restored.

The New Testament believer is no longer enslaved to the power of sin.

In Romans 6:14, Paul verifies why *"sin"* (the power of sin) is no longer *"master"* over the New Testament believer. *"Sin"* holds no mastery because we are *"not under law, but under grace."* No doubt, the power of sin responds intriguingly to *"law."* It gains strength! In other words, its power intensifies. Thus, before we were saved, the harder we strove to keep the Law, the more the power of sin increased in strength. Finally, when the Law had accomplished its purpose, we saw while depraved our need for a Savior, surrendered to Christ, and were justified (saved) by the God of *"grace."* It was then that we began living under *"grace,"* and sin's power was broken. The power of *"sin"* can still *"reign in"* our *"body"* (Romans 6:12), but only when we are caught off guard. In fact, we commit acts of sin because we choose to sin, not because it is natural for us to do so. This topic will be discussed in more depth when we study Romans 7.

Paul next presents a question that his enemies frequently posed:

> *What then? Shall we sin because we are not under law, but under grace?...*
> (Romans 6:15)

Paul's critics not only rejected his theology, but accused him of granting believers a license to sin (much the same as in Romans 6:1). Paul again uses the strong Greek expression, *"May it never be"* (Romans 6:15), proving that these accusations were totally unjustified. After all, he later wrote (in Colossians 3:25) that we suffer consequences in this life from the sins committed as believers. Paul makes a statement in Romans 6:16 that forever settles the issue. He points out that we, as believers, are the *"slaves of the one"* we *"obey,"* whether it is *"sin,"* which leads to *"death,"* or *"obedience,"* which results *"in righteousness."* If *"sin"* brings *"death,"* why would Paul preach a gospel that promotes disobedience? He couldn't, and that is his point! Note: The word *"death,"* as it relates to New Testament believers, can point to physical death as in 1Corinthians 11:30 and other similar passages. It can also describe the emptiness experienced by believers while walking in unconfessed sin. That sin can cause believers to live as though they are dead for short seasons of time is undeniable, but as was the case with David, once repentance and confession are exercised, a zest for life is restored.

While we were without Christ, we *"...were slaves of sin..."* (Romans 6:17). We loved sin, basked in sin, submerged ourselves in sin, sinned in many ways and on a variety of occasions. We did so because we were the old self, and sin came as natural as breathing. This doesn't mean that we were incapable of repenting and believing while depraved, but rather that we were sin's slave so long as we refused to repent and exercise faith. We will discover shortly that we as believers are slaves of righteousness, yet sometimes sin. Therefore, we are capable of responding contrary to our strongest inclination, a subject that will be examined in more depth in Romans 7.

Paul, in Romans 6:17, continues by writing: *"...you became obedient from the heart..."* Some individuals who have not become *"obedient from the heart"* claim to know Christ and are, therefore, lost. Why so? All who are born of God's Spirit receive a new *"heart,"* a new nature, and desire to obey their Master. As a result, they possess a transformed attitude regarding sin. Without question, a person who has *"become obedient from the heart"* experiences a radical change of lifestyle.

When we became *"obedient from the heart"* (Romans 6:17), we were *"freed from"* both the power and penalty of *"sin"* (Romans 6:18). We also *"became slaves of righteousness"* (Romans 6:18). Be sure to understand Paul's point here. The power of sin can control us only if we are caught off guard, for we have become *"slaves of righteousness"* due to our new nature. Consequently, the *"members"* of our body should behave more righteously—not as they behaved prior to our being made new (Romans 6:19).

Did you notice the last phrase of Romans 6:19—*"resulting in sanctification"*? Paul states that if we *"present"* the *"members"* of our bodies *"as slaves to righteousness"* (on an ongoing basis), then *"sanctification"* results. We studied in Week 7 (Romans 5:1), however, that our spirits and souls were sanctified (made holy and perfect) the moment we were justified/saved. Is Romans 6:19 a contradiction? Of course not! In verse 19, Paul is saying that we will progressively live out in our experiences what has already taken place in our spirits and souls. In other words, we will start to behave in a more sanctified (holy) manner due to having already been sanctified in our spirits and souls at the point of justification/salvation. Hebrews 10:14 addresses this subject as well as any verse in the Scriptures. It says:

> *For by one offering He has perfected for all time those who are* <u>*are sanctified*</u> [being sanctified]. (Hebrews 10:14 NASB)

> *Because by one sacrifice he has made perfect forever those who are* <u>*being made holy*</u> (Hebrews 10:14 NIV)

Note that the word *"sanctified"* in the NASB actually means "being sanctified." Therefore, the NIV's rendering is, *"being made holy,"* since the terms *"holy"* and *"sanctified"* are synonymous. Yes, our souls and spirits are made perfect forever at the point of justification, but our behavior is *"being made holy"* on an ongoing basis. Thus, you can be perfect and holy (sanctified) in your person

We are not on a performance-based acceptance with God.

before your behavior lines up with who you are. Isn't it wonderful to know that we are not on a performance-based acceptance with God, and that what we sometimes do (when we commit acts of sin) is not who we are? In other words, if you tell a lie, you are not a liar. You are a saint who has told a lie, for you have acted in an unnatural manner. Believe me, a tremendous difference exists in these two mind-sets. In fact, what we do is not who we are, even though who we are has a tremendous impact on what we do.

We were without *"righteousness"* while in our lost state (Romans 6:20), *"deriving"* no *"benefit...from the things of which we are now ashamed"*—grossly ashamed (Romans 6:21). *"But now having been freed from sin and enslaved to God"* [being enslaved to God means that you desire to serve Him with all your heart], we *"derive"* the *"benefit"* of *"sanctification"* and *"eternal life"* (Romans 6:22). Great news isn't it?!

As was discussed earlier, to be *"enslaved to God"* does not mean that we cease sinning now that we are believers. We will commit sin to the grave, although we were *"freed from"* the power of *"sin"* the moment we believed (Romans 6:22). Consequently, just as being *"enslaved to God"* does not mean that we totally cease responding to the power of sin's influence, being enslaved to sin in our lost state did not mean that we were incapable of exercising repentance and faith while depraved. Make sure to digest the content of this paragraph before proceeding.

We can now shout at the top of our voices Paul's words of Romans 6:23:

> For the wages of sin is death, but the free gift of God is eternal life in Christ Jesus our Lord. (Romans 6:23)

*B*eing enslaved to sin in our lost state did not mean that we were incapable of exercising repentance and faith while depraved.

No doubt, *"the wages of sin is death,"* but did you notice that God's *"free gift...is eternal life,"* and that this *"life"* is found in *"Jesus"*? We should be motivated, therefore, to communicate these wonderful truths to anyone and everyone who will listen. I need to warn you, however. God must instruct you in how to say what is addressed here before you begin instructing others. Many have jumped the gun and suffered horrendous consequences. Once you are ready, God will see to it that you have ample opportunity to spread this magnificent news to a hurting and dying world.

You will enjoy next week's lesson. It will exhibit more of the practical side of what we have been discussing. Enjoy your day off, but come back ready to be encouraged.

Romans 7 Questions

Make sure to ask the Lord for understanding throughout the week. The truths in this chapter can revolutionize our entire Christian experience.

First Day

1. Read Romans 7:1-25. What do verses 1-4 teach regarding our relationship to *"the Law"*? How is a person released from *"the Law"* (v.4)?

2. How do Galatians 2:20 and Romans 6:6 relate to Romans 7:4?

Second Day

Read Romans 7:5. It is imperative to note that the phrase *"in the flesh"* in the New American Standard Bible (NASB) is interpreted "controlled by the sinful nature" in the New International Version (NIV). In fact, the NIV takes the liberty to render the word *"flesh"(sarx)* as "sinful nature" in Romans 7:5, 7:18, 7:25, 8:3, 8:4, 8:5, 8:8, 8:9, 8:12, and 8:13. The correct rendering is *"flesh."* The King James, New King James, Revised Standard, Modern, Amplified, New American Standard—even the Greek Interlinear—use *"flesh"* instead of "sinful nature." No doubt, some copies of the NIV have the word "flesh" recorded in the margins, but I have found that most people don't read the margins. Thus, many believers who read Romans 7 and 8 in the NIV come away with the idea that they are dual natured—both old self and new self, both cat and hog.

We learned in Romans 6:6 that the sinful nature has been eradicated in a New Testament believer. Because Romans 7 and 8 address the experiences of a New Testament believer, the correct translation is *"flesh"* and not "sinful nature." Evidently, the editors of the NIV accepted the idea of Positional Truth—that the New Testament believer is dual natured—both old self and new self. If both natures are alive in us, we are living in spiritual adultery, as verified by Romans 7:1-4.

The NIV also used the phrases, "The mind of sinful man," and, "the sinful mind," in Romans 8:6-7. The correct rendering in both cases is *"the mind set on the flesh."* Therefore, when we read Romans 7 and 8, we must keep in mind what has been discussed here. As was stated in the introduction of the course, I use the New American Standard Bible, which has served me extremely well.

1. Read Romans 7:1-25. When Paul uses the phrase *"in the flesh"* (v.5), to what is he referring? We will examine this phrase in detail while studying Romans 8. Consequently, if you have difficulty answering this question, don't be overly concerned.

2.   What arouses *"the sinful passions"* (affections) in an unbeliever (v.5)?   What does this verify regarding the purpose of *"the Law"*?   List other verses that communicate the same basic truth concerning the Law.

3.   How is a person *"released from the Law"* (v.6)?   If you are a believer, when did you die, and what part of you *"died"*?   What does it mean to *"serve in newness of the Spirit and not in oldness of the letter"*?

Third Day

1.   Read Romans 7:1-25.   What is stated about *"the Law"* in Romans 7:7?   Have you noticed the number of times that Paul has mentioned the purpose of the Law?   He certainly wasn't fearful of being redundant, was he?

2.   In Romans 7:8-11, the word *"sin"* refers to the power of sin.   What occurs when the power of *"sin"* is exposed to *"the Law."*   Tie this in with what we discussed in association with Romans 6:14.   Can you see the necessity of living by *"grace"* rather than *"Law"*?   Are you living by *"grace"*?   What can you expect if you choose to remain under *"Law"* as a New Testament believer?   According to Galatians 3:1-3, how did Paul view the believers at Galatia who chose to remain under Law?

Fourth Day

1.   Read Romans 7:1-25.   What does Paul mean by the statement: *"...the Law is holy, and the commandment is holy and righteous and good"* (v.12)?   What happened in Paul when the Law and the power of *"sin"* met (v.13)?   Have you had this same experience at any time in the past?   If so, when?   Considering what we have discussed, explain in more detail why *"the Law is holy"* (v.12).   It is imperative that we comprehend the purpose of the Law.

2.   Verses 14-17 describe the battle that rages in every New Testament believer. Is this battle between the old self and the new self (new man)? If not, who (or what) is involved in the battle?

3.   According to Romans 7:17, what did Paul discover about the power of *"sin"*? The following is an extremely difficult question, so don't be discouraged if the answer escapes you. To what does the word *"it"* refer in Romans 7:17?

Fifth Day

1.   Read Romans 7:1-25. In Romans 7:18-20, Paul again describes the battle that raged within him as a believer. What does Paul mean when he says, *"For I know that nothing good dwells in me, that is, in my flesh..."*? To properly interpret this statement, we must remember that the power of sin dwells in a New Testament believer's flesh (physical body). Paul is not saying, however, that his physical body is evil. Note: The word *"flesh"* in Romans 7:18 is referring to the physical body. It can refer to something else as well, as will be confirmed next week.

2.   How does verse 20 tie in with verse 17? To what does the word *"it"* refer in verse 20?

Sixth Day

1.   Read Romans 7:1-25. From what is stated in Romans 7:21-23, where does *"the law of "sin"* reside (live) in a New Testament believer? Note: The phrase *"law of sin"* points to the power of sin. What does the *"law of sin,"* or power of sin, wage *"war against"* in the New Testament believer (v.23)? This section is one of the most difficult of the study, so take your time.

2.   The word *"Wretched"* in verse 24 means "distressed" or "miserable." No doubt, Paul was far from viewing himself as *"Wretched"* in the sense of being worthless. After all, the apostle understood well that he was a saint who sometimes sinned—not a lowly sinner saved by grace. Thus, he was distressed over the battle that raged in his mind as a result of the power of sin working through the avenue of his *"body"* (*"the body of this death"*—verse 24). Through what means did Paul find deliverance (vv.24-25)? What does the last sentence of Romans 7:25 communicate to you? Don't forget that the phrase *"law of sin"* means "power of sin." Enjoy this week's lesson, and digest as much of it as possible. It is one of the most important lessons in the entire course.

Romans 7 Lesson

I had heard for years that Romans 7 describes the defeated Christian. One day, I realized it does just the opposite. I found, in fact, that it reveals the source of the conflict within every New Testament believer and at the same time explains the way to victory.

When I read Romans 7 as a new believer, I became more aware of my own struggles. I wasn't mature enough, however, to understand the source of those struggles. I thought if I could feed the old self (Adamic nature, old man, dead spirit, sinful nature) enough truth and whip him into line, the battle would subside. I did not yet comprehend that my old self had been crucified and made extinct. I soon learned, nonetheless, that the intensity of the battle did not decrease as my Biblical knowledge increased. In fact, I found that the battle intensified as I matured in my walk with Christ. It was then that I discovered a life-changing truth. I learned that my struggle is with the power of sin and not with my old self (Adamic nature). This insight brought new hope and, with it, a greater desire to live life by Christ's life within me. In other words, I was free to explore what it means to live life by the life of Another, the life of my Savior.

Our understanding of spiritual warfare will be enhanced through this week's lesson. Don't be surprised, therefore, if the intensity of the battle increases as we study this chapter. Satan will do everything within his power to prevent us from seeing this truth, so pray for wisdom before continuing.

You will find that I repeat myself throughout this lesson. In other words, I will say the same thing in different ways. Know that this repetition is done with purpose in mind. In teaching these truths over the years, I have found it to be a necessity.

Released from Law through Death

Paul first addresses the means by which we are released from the Law, and he uses the marriage relationship to prove his point (vv.1-4). In marriage, death of one of the partners automatically frees the surviving partner to remarry. What is Paul's point? In our lost state, we were joined (in a sense, married) to the Law. Because the Law will live forever (1Peter 1:25), our release could be achieved through one avenue only, through our own personal death. As was verified earlier on, our death (the death of the old self) occurred on the cross (Romans 7:4; Galatians 2:20; Romans 6:6) through being placed in Christ subsequent to our repenting and believing while depraved (review the lesson associated with Romans 6:1-6, Part 2). Thus, it is permissible for us to be *"joined to"* Christ, for the old self is dead and gone. Otherwise, our betrothal to Christ would be an impossibility. Should the old self remain alive, living alongside the new self, the old self would be married to the Law at the same time that the new self is betrothed to Christ. Spiritual adultery would result, creating a situation that is totally irreconcilable. Yet many view the New Testament believer as dual natured, possessing both the old and new self. Do you see the contradiction associated with such thinking?

*M*y struggle is with the power of sin and *not* with my old self (Adamic nature).

As a result of being *"joined to another,"* we can *"bear fruit for God"* through living by the life of *"another,"* the *"another"* being Jesus Himself (Romans 7:4) who is *"God"* (Hebrews 1:8).

From Romans 7:5, we see that *"...while we were in the flesh* [in our lost condition], *the sinful passions* [affections]*...were aroused by the Law..."* These *"passions...were aroused"* because the power of sin increases in intensity when exposed to *"the Law."* Consequently, the more we worked at keeping the Law, the more we broke it. We were constantly bearing *"fruit for death,"* that is, producing the fruit of an unbeliever. Don't misunderstand. Paul is not teaching that the depraved are incapable of recognizing their sin and exercising repentance and faith, for Adam realized he was *"naked"* after eating of the forbidden fruit and dying a spiritual death (Genesis 2:16-17; Genesis 3:7). For more input regarding this subject, you can obtain a copy of our series titled, *God's Heart: As it Relates to Depravity,* distributed by this ministry.

Good news is on the horizon, for Romans 7:6 confirms that *"...we have been released from the Law..."* through our death with Christ. This teaching is in total agreement with Romans 6:6, which verifies *"...that our old self was crucified with Him..."* The death of the *"old self"* frees us to *"...serve in newness of the Spirit and not in oldness of the letter"* of *"the Law"* (Romans 7:6). Yes, we are free to allow the *"Spirit"* of God to provide victory over anything that comes our way. What freedom!

We should take courage from Romans 7:7, for as Paul was accused of teaching error we will be accused of the same. His enemies struggled with his theology, making statements such as, "Paul, if what you are teaching is true, the Law must be sin." Paul disagreed by responding with, *"May it never be!"* He went ahead to say that had it not been for *"the Law"* he *"would not have known about coveting."* *"Coveting"* is a sin that can be hidden from the unbeliever, but not from the Law. Had the Law not been present to expose Paul's sin, he would have continued in his self-righteousness, never seeing his need for a Savior.

In Romans 7:8-11, Paul confirms that the power of *"sin"* increases in intensity when exposed to the Law. Realizing that this increase would occur, God gave the Law so we might recognize our sinful and depraved state through our increased involvement with sin. It is for this reason that Paul writes:

> *for sin, taking opportunity through the commandment, deceived me, and through it killed me.* (Romans 7:11)

No doubt, *"the Law is holy"* (Romans 7:12); it serves the purpose for which it was given. It makes *"sin...utterly sinful"* (Romans 7:13), doing its job and doing it well.

The Battle Between the New Testament Believer and the Power of Sin

Romans 7:14-17 speaks of the battle that occurs inside every New Testament believer. We want to do good, but at times we find ourselves doing evil. Certainly, the power of sin comes against all church saints. But through what avenue does it launch its attack? If we can answer correctly, we are well on our way to victory. The answer is contained in verse 17.

Paul, in verse 17, describes a major turning point in his earlier walk with Christ.

> *So now, no longer am I the one doing it, but sin which indwells me.* (Romans 7:17).

Paul came to the realization that the sinful thoughts entering his mind were not generated by the old self (Adamic nature) but were the work of the power of sin living in his physical body. Until that time, he had assumed that the old self was alive, producing the evil thoughts that bombarded his thinking. He discovered, however, that the old self is dead and gone in a New Testament believer, never to be reckoned with again. This eradication means that the battle raging inside us is between the power of sin and the new self, not between the old self and the new self. How can a battle exist between the old self and the new self when the old self no longer exists?

So long as we allow the power of sin to trick us into believing that the old self is still alive, it can convince us that we are generating the evil thoughts that bombard our

The battle raging inside us is between the power of sin and the new self, not between the old self and the new self.

minds. Only through understanding that the old self has been eradicated and that the sinful thoughts are generated by the power of sin <u>living in our body</u> can we take authority over the power of sin (through the power of the Holy Spirit) and walk in victory. Understanding this truth radically changed Paul's experience as a New Testament believer. My prayer is that it will do the same for us. A quick review of the circle diagrams might be helpful at this time.

One more point regarding Romans 7:17 and we will move on. Initially reading this passage seems to suggest that Paul is teaching that he (the new self) did not commit sin. Such cannot be true, for 1John 1:8 states:

> *If we say we have no sin, we are deceiving ourselves, and the truth is not in us.*
> (1John 1:8)

Paul is <u>not</u> advocating that he no longer sinned, but that the power of sin is the initiator and source of the evil thoughts that penetrate the New Testament believer's mind.

Verses 18-19 are similar to verses 14-15, for Paul focuses on the battle generated by the power of sin living in his *"flesh"* (body). As has already been determined, he realized that the initiator of the evil is *"sin,"* the power of *"sin,"* as verified by verse 20 as well:

> *But if I am doing the very thing I do not wish, I am no longer the one doing it, but* <u>*sin*</u> *which dwells in me.* (Romans 7:20)

Considering what we have discussed, we can view verse 20 as follows:

> *"But if I am doing the very thing I do not wish, I am no longer the one producing the evil thoughts that wage war against my mind, for they are produced by the power of sin which dwells in my body."*

Do you comprehend how this wonderful truth affects our walk with Christ? It means that through the power of the Holy Spirit we can catch the power of sin at its game and refuse whatever it sends our way. Because the new self is incapable of producing such thoughts (even though the new self is capable of committing sin) and since the *"old self"* has been eradicated (Romans 6:6), we can *"consider"* ourselves *"dead"* to these thoughts (Romans 6:11), living in victory through God's life within (Romans 6:13).

The power of sin is the initiator and source of the evil thoughts that penetrate the New Testament believer's mind.

The phrase, *"But if I am doing the very thing I do not wish..."* (Romans 7:20), confirms that Paul, as a New Testament believer, sometimes responded against (contrary to) his strongest inclination. We do the same when we walk in sin, for our strongest inclination is to walk in righteousness. In fact, should you place the new man in a temptation-free environment, he would never sin. Thus, when we eject out of our earthly bodies and are taken to heaven, we will walk in sinless perfection. Why? Our strongest inclination as holy and blameless saints is to obey. When we sin, therefore, we are walking contrary to our strongest inclination. It is worth noting that those who view the depraved as incapable of exercising personal repentance and faith teach that man cannot respond against (contrary to) his strongest inclination. Paul proves such thinking invalid.

Paul made a great discovery. He discovered that *"evil"* was *"present"* in him, even though he wished *"to do good"* (Romans 7:21). The *"evil"* spoken of here is the power of sin which lived in his body. It is an organized power and must remain as that—it is <u>not</u> a demon. Also, he *"joyfully"* concurred *"with the law of God in the inner man"* (Romans 7:22), *"law"* meaning principle—not Mosaic Law. In other words, he desired to walk with God to the greatest degree possible. He, however, had a problem: A *"law"* (or principle—the power of sin) lived *"in the members of"* his *"body,"* which waged *"war against"* his *"mind,"* and made him *"a prisoner of the law of sin"* (power of sin) which was in the *"members"* of his body (Romans 7:23).

Was his condition hopeless? Of course not according to Romans 7:24-25! *"Jesus Christ"* had set him *"free from the body of this death,"* from having to be controlled by the power of sin as it worked through his physical *"body."* He was *"free,"* therefore, to reject sin's lie *"through"* the authority and power of *"Jesus Christ our Lord."* The choice was his, for every New Testament believer has the option of walking according to God's truth and strength or according to the enemy's (sin's) lies. We will discuss this freedom in great detail in Romans 8.

Deliverance through Christ Alone

Some people have wrestled with Paul's description of himself in Romans 7:24. They question why he would refer to himself as *"wretched"* when he taught elsewhere that his *"old self"* was *"crucified"* (Romans 6:6), that he was *"a new creation"* (2Corinthians 5:17), in fact, a *"holy and blameless"* (Ephesians 1:4) *"saint"* (1Corinthians 1:2). This concern is easily diffused. The word *"wretched"* in this case actually means *"distressed"* or *"miserable."* Paul was not saying that he was a *"wretched"* person in the sense of being worthless. After all, he knew well that he was a saint who sometimes sinned, not a worthless, wretched sinner. He was basically communicating his frustration over the battle that raged in his mind due to the power of sin working through his *"body," "the body of this death"* (v.24). He found victory, however, through Jesus' life within (v.25).

> *Every believer has the option of walking according to God's truth and strength or according to the enemy's (sin's) lies.*

Romans 7 – The Victorious Christian's Chapter

Romans 7 does anything but describe the defeated Christian. In fact, it explains how a New Testament believer can (through Christ's indwelling presence) experience victory over the power of sin! Paul realized that the evil thoughts bombarding his mind were not self-generated, but were produced by the power of sin <u>disguising itself as the old self</u>. If the power of sin can convince us that the old self is still alive, we will view ourselves as part evil and part good and, in turn, as lowly sinners saved by grace. As a result, we will be unable to appropriate our true identity (the fact that we are saints who through Christ have authority over the power of sin) and will live in defeat. Yes, deception is one of our enemy's most powerful weapons.

We will dig deeper into these truths next week, so come back ready to be blessed.

Romans 8:1-11 Questions

First Day

Romans 8 will add depth to what we have previously addressed. We will use this truth the remainder of our lives, so digest everything you can from this wonderful chapter.

1.   Read Romans 8:1-11. Why could Paul teach that *"There is therefore now no condemnation for those who are in Christ Jesus"* (Romans 8:1)? Be sure to answer this question as thoroughly as possible.

2.   Why should Romans 8:1 enhance our fellowship with the Father? Has it helped you deal more effectively with your sin? If so, how?

Second Day

1.   Read Romans 8:1-11. The word *"law"* in Romans 8:2 actually means "principle." Taking this into account, what does Paul mean when he writes, *"For the law of the Spirit of life in Christ Jesus has set you free from the law of sin and death"*? Be sure to factor in what we have been studying regarding the power of sin.

2.   What was the Mosaic *"Law"* incapable of doing (v.3)? To answer correctly, you will need to focus on what was discussed in earlier lessons.

3.   Keeping in mind the previous question and continuing to deal with Romans 8:3, what did God do as a result of this weakness in the Mosaic Law? What did this action condemn?

4.   What does the phrase, *"He condemned sin in the flesh,"* communicate to you? As you answer this question, take into consideration what we have been discussing regarding the power of sin and where it dwells. Also, understand that the word *"flesh,"* depending on the context, can refer to: (1) The physical body which is flesh (2) The ungodly habit patterns lodged in the brain—the brain being part of the fleshly body.

Third Day

1.   Read Romans 8:1-11. In Romans 8:4, Paul describes how *"the requirement of the Law"* can be *"fulfilled"* in our lives. How is this done?

2.   Remember that the word *"flesh"* can refer to: (1) The body (which is flesh) (2) The ungodly habit patterns lodged in our brain, the brain being a piece of flesh. Consequently, when we *"walk according to the flesh"* (v.4), we have believed the power of sin's lie and responded to one of our ungodly habit patterns etched in the brain. Make sure to take advantage of Circle Diagram 7. If someone asked you to explain the phrase, *"walk according to the flesh,"* how would you answer?

3.   Refer to Circle Diagram 8. What does Paul mean by the phrase, *"…walk…according to the Spirit"* (v.4)? How does Romans 8:5 relate to this topic?

Fourth Day

1.   Read Romans 8:1-11. In Romans 8:6-7, Paul describes what occurs when we *"set"* our minds on either *"the flesh"* or *"the Spirit."* What results? Take into consideration what was stated about the *"flesh"* in the second question of yesterday's lesson.

2.   When we set our minds on *"the flesh,"* what have we incorrectly allowed to happen in our thought processes? (Refer to Circle Diagram 7.)

Fifth Day

1.   Read Romans 8:1-11. What does it mean to be *"in the flesh"* (vv.8-9)? How does a person move from being *"in the flesh"* to being *"in the Spirit"* (v.9)? A person who is *"in the flesh cannot please God"* (v.8). Why can't the depraved *"please God"* so long as they refuse to choose to believe?

Sixth Day

1.   Read Romans 8:1-11. What does Paul mean in verse 10 when he writes, *"the body is dead because of sin"*? What does he mean when he writes, *"the spirit is alive because of righteousness"*? If you had difficulty answering these two questions, this week's lesson should benefit you greatly.

2.   According to Romans 8:11, God's *"Spirit...dwells in"* the New Testament believer. The Father uses Him for a specific purpose once He *"dwells in"* us. What is that purpose?

3.   How has learning (or reviewing) this encouraged you today? Have you noticed that Paul uses much of what he teaches in Romans 1-7 as he explains himself in Romans 8:1-11?

Romans 8:1-11 Lesson

No Condemnation

Has there been a time when a condemning thought ran through your mind, a thought that condemned your person? (If you are human, your answer should be "yes!") Did you believe the thought? Did it cause you to <u>feel</u> discouraged and inadequate? If so, great news is on the horizon! Christ's death, burial, and resurrection occurred that we might, along with many other things, realize that *"There is therefore now no condemnation for those who are in Christ Jesus"* (Romans 8:1). Thus, any thought that condemns your person is invalid and can be totally disregarded.

It is imperative to remember that Satan condemns the <u>believer</u>, the believer's person, while the Holy Spirit condemns only the <u>behavior</u> of the believer when necessary. For instance, suppose I should tell a lie. On the heels of that lie, the power of sin will probably generate the thought, "I am nothing but a worthless liar" (note the first person pronoun "I"). And, moreover, it will do so in a tone of voice, including accent and dialect, that sounds just like mine. It will condemn <u>me</u>, my person. The Holy Spirit, however, will say, "I hate lying, but you remain the apple of my eye." Do you see the difference? No doubt, Romans 8:1 is wonderful ammunition against the power of sin's schemes.

Unlike the King James and the New King James, we find that the New American Standard, the New International, the Phillips Translation, the Ryrie Study Bible, along with other versions, do not include the phrase "who walk not after the flesh, but after the Spirit."

> *There is therefore now no condemnation to them which are in Christ Jesus, <u>who</u> <u>walk not after the flesh, but after the Spirit.</u>* (Romans 8:1 KJV—emphasis added)

> *There is therefore now no condemnation for those who are in Christ Jesus.*
> (Romans 8:1 NASB)

Neither is this phrase found in the most ancient manuscripts accessible today. As a result, it is not included in the text of the more recent versions.

Because *"There is...now no condemnation for those who are in Christ Jesus"* (Romans 8:1), we have the freedom to deal with our acts of sin the instant we commit them. No more putting them off. No more excuses. The Father is waiting for us to repent and confess so fellowship can be restored, not so He might forgive us, for we are already forgiven. Many church saints put off confessing their sin because they wrongly believe that condemnation awaits them.

Set Free through Christ Jesus

Paul goes ahead to say that *"...the law of the Spirit of life in Christ Jesus has set you free from the law of sin and of death"* (v.2). The word *"law"* means "principle" rather than Mosaic Law. Consequently, *"the principle of the Spirit of life in Christ Jesus has set you free from the principle* [or power] *of sin and of death."* No doubt, those who walk by God's *"Spirit"* are guaranteed deliverance from the principle (or power) of *"sin."*

*T*here is therefore now no condemnation for those who are in Christ Jesus" (Romans 8:1).

Romans 8:3 makes an intriguing statement: *"For what the Law could not do, weak as it was through the flesh, God did..."* It is obvious that *"the Law"* cannot save a person from God's condemnation, while the cross and Christ's subsequent resurrection can.

God sent His Son as an offering for sin, an action that removed our sin nature and forgave our sins once we exercised repentance and faith while depraved. This offering also released us from our enslavement to the power of sin. Thus, God *"condemned sin in the flesh"*—that is, the power of *"sin"* which dwells in the New Testament believer's body (v.3). This truth fits perfectly with our previous observations.

The Power of God's Spirit

Let's take a moment to address an extremely important issue. Without a doubt, *"the Law is holy"* (Romans 7:12) and cannot be kept through one's own power, discipline, or strength. An amazing transformation occurs, however, when we exercise repentance and faith while depraved and the Holy Spirit invades our spirit to make us new. Paul teaches that *"...the requirement of the Law"* is

> *The Spirit of God, when released to control our lives, will empower us to walk a path consistent with the moral standard of the Law.*

"fulfilled in us, who do not walk according to the flesh, but according to the Spirit" (Romans 8:4). Do you realize that? The Spirit of God, when released to control our lives, will empower us to walk a path consistent with the moral standard of the Law. God, in turn, receives all the credit and glory; we in the process learn the true meaning of life.

Walking According to the Flesh Versus the Spirit

It is imperative that two phrases from Romans 8:4 be understood. The first phrase is *"walk according to the flesh."* The second is *"walk...according to the Spirit."* Both refer to a particular state of a New Testament believer. The latter is easily understood, for walking *"according to the Spirit"* occurs when we allow the Spirit of God to control our behavior (Circle Diagram 8). To *"walk according to the flesh,"* however, means to allow ungodly habit patterns stored in the brain, the brain being a piece of *"flesh,"* to influence our behavior. We do so when we believe the power of sin's lie sent into our minds by means of these ungodly patterns. We must understand that all ungodly habit patterns are not removed at the point of justification. Realize as well that new ungodly habits are formed when we allow the new self (new man) to be controlled by the power of sin in a new area of sinful behavior.

Paul continues in Romans 8:5 by writing:

> *For those who are according to the flesh set their minds on the things of the flesh...* (Romans 8:5)

You are walking *"according to the flesh"* if you *"set"* you mind on sin's message (conveyed through the avenue of an ungodly habit pattern in the brain—which is a piece of flesh) and respond by acting on the message (Circle Diagram 7). It is then that the new man sins.

Paul also teaches that those walking *"according to the Spirit"* set their *"minds"* on *"the things of the Spirit"* (Romans 8:5). In this case, the new man is walking in obedience (reference Circle Diagram 8). Sounds pretty simple, doesn't it? But it can certainly be difficult in practice.

To *"set"* our minds *"on the flesh is death,"* but to *"set"* our minds *"on the Spirit is life and peace"* (Romans 8:6). Paul follows in Romans 8:7 by writing:

> *because the mind set on the flesh is hostile toward God; for it does not subject itself to the law* [principle] *of God, for it is not even able to do so;* (Romans 8:7)

Yes, a New Testament believer who is walking *"according to the flesh"* will behave much like an unbeliever, even act in a *"hostile"* manner *"toward God"*—but he is never at peace while doing so. How can a cat enjoy wallowing in a mud hole?! Impossible!

Paul next addresses what it means to be *"in the flesh"* versus *"in the Spirit"* (Romans 8:8-9). A person who is *"in the flesh cannot please God":*

> *and those who are in the flesh cannot please God.* (Romans 8:8)

Thus, to be *"in the flesh"* is to be lost. We are *"in the Spirit"* and saved, however, *if...the Spirit of God dwells in"* us (Romans 8:9):

> *...But if anyone does not have the Spirit of Christ, he does not belong to Him.*
> (Romans 8:9)

No doubt, *"those who are in the flesh"* (v.8) do not *"belong"* to God because they are void of the *"Spirit of Christ"* (v.9). Only those who repent and believe while depraved can receive the *"Spirit."*

With the above in mind, can you understand the difference between being *"in the flesh"* and walking *"according to the flesh"*? The first phrase, *"in the flesh,"* refers to a person who does not know Christ. The second, walking *"according to the flesh,"* refers to those times when a New Testament believer gives in to an ungodly habit pattern due to believing the power of sin's lie. As has already been established, the power of sin dwells in the New Testament believer's body and sends messages into the mind by means of the ungodly habit patterns stored in the brain, which is a piece of *"flesh."*

The power of sin dwells in the New Testament believer's body and sends messages into the mind by means of the ungodly habit patterns stored in the brain.

In Romans 8:10, Paul stresses that in relation to a New Testament believer, *"...the body is dead because of sin..."* Paul is not teaching that our bodies cease functioning after accepting Jesus as Savior. He proves, rather, that we can consider powerless any lie that the power of *"sin"* sends into our minds through the avenue of *"the body."* This teaching ties in perfectly with our discussion regarding Romans 6:11, so you might want to review that lesson. (Note: It is the power of sin's thought that enters the New Testament believer's mind, not the power of sin itself.)

Paul also stresses that *"...the spirit is alive because of righteousness"* (Romans 8:10). In other words, because we know Christ and are *"righteous,"* our *"spirit is alive."* After all, we are *"one spirit with...the Lord"* (1Corinthians 6:17), making us *"alive"* indeed (Romans 8:10).

Paul is not finished, for he confirms that God's *"Spirit"* living inside us gives *"life to"* our *"mortal bodies"* (Romans 8:11).

> *But if the Spirit of Him who raised Jesus from the dead dwells in you, He who raised Christ Jesus from the dead will also give life to your mortal bodies through His Spirit who indwells you.* (Romans 8:11)

The apostle is making reference to more than receiving our glorified bodies at the Rapture of the church. He is also speaking of the privilege we now have of living above our temptations through the power of the Holy Spirit. God did more than deliver us from condemnation through justification—subsequent to our repenting and believing while depraved. He also empowers our lives in the here and now as we yield to His life within us. Remember: Christ's blood is the avenue through which our sins were removed; His body is the avenue through which our old self was eradicated. Consequently, we were freed from the penalty of sin through Jesus' blood, but we have been freed from the dominion of the power of sin through our death with Jesus on the cross. What great news! Isn't Romans a phenomenal book?

Romans 8:12-25 Questions

First Day

1. Read Romans 8:1-25. Note the phrase, *"live according to the flesh,"* in Romans 8:12-13. Considering previous lessons, to what does this phrase refer?

2. A review of last week's lesson will assist you in answering this next question. What is the difference between *"living according to the flesh"* and being *"in the flesh"?*

3. From Romans 8:12-13, what results when we choose to *"live according to the flesh"?*

4. Explain the phrase, *"but if by the Spirit you are putting to death the deeds of the body"* (v.13). What results when we put *"to death the deeds of the body"* by means of God's *"Spirit"* (v.13)?

5. When you call on the *"Spirit"* to put *"to death the deeds of the body,"* what type of thought process have you found to be most effective?

Second Day

1. Read Romans 8:12-25. In Romans 8:14 we find the statement, *"For all who are being led by the Spirit of God, these are sons of God."* What does it mean to be *"led by the Spirit of God"?* If you want, you can explain this in terms of what you have gleaned from the circle diagrams.

2. According to Romans 8:15, New Testament believers *"have received"* something very special. What is it?

3. If God is your *"Father"* (v.15), how do you view Him? Is your view based on what the Scriptures say about Him, or is it based on what you have experienced in your relationship with your earthly father?

4. The type of *"spirit"* that a New Testament believer does <u>not</u> receive is also addressed in verse 15. Describe this *"spirit"* in your own words. Again, what type of *"spirit"* does a New Testament believer receive?

5. In your opinion, what, more than anything else, keeps the majority of the lost from choosing God as their *"Father"?*

Third Day

1. Read Romans 8:12-25. One of the assets of possessing the *"Spirit"* is mentioned in Romans 8:16. What is that asset?

2. What excites you most about being a child of God?

3. We are *"…heirs of God and fellow heirs with Christ…"* (Romans 8:17). What does this mean?

4. How can suffering in the here and now help prepare us for future glory (v.17)?

Fourth Day

1. Read Romans 8:12-25. As you read Romans 8:18, try to understand Paul's view of suffering. What allowed him to walk in victory?

2. What adjectives did Paul use in 2Corinthians 4:17 to describe his affliction? What was his suffering producing? Compare this with Paul's words in Romans 8:18.

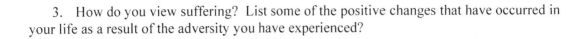

3.   How do you view suffering? List some of the positive changes that have occurred in your life as a result of the adversity you have experienced?

4.   If you are presently walking in a difficult situation, take time to thank the Lord for your pain. Also thank Him for using it to teach you more about the cross.

Fifth Day

1.   Read Romans 8:12-25. Now read Romans 8:19-22 a second time. Why does *"the creation"* wait *"eagerly for the revealing of the sons of God"?*

2.   When was *"the creation"* cursed? Do you view *"the creation"* as being in *"slavery to corruption"* (v.21)? Considering that the earth is now cursed, take a moment to imagine its original state.

3.   At some point in the future the earth will be released from its curse. When will this take place? Isaiah 30:23-26, Isaiah 35:1-2, and Ezekiel 36:28-38 describe some of the conditions that will exist during that time period. Write down any new insights below.

Sixth Day

1.   Read Romans 8:12-25. We, as church saints, *"groan within ourselves"* (Romans 8:23). Why? How does Paul define the phrase, *"our adoption as sons,"* in verse 23?

2.   Read Romans 8:24-25, 2Corinthians 4:17-18, and Hebrews 11:27. How can viewing the *"unseen"* (Hebrews 11:27) assist us during times of intense suffering?

3.   Has studying this encouraged you to know Christ more intimately? Explain.

Romans 8:12-25 Lesson

Not Obligated to Sin

Isn't it wonderful to know that, *"There is therefore now no condemnation for those who are in Christ Jesus"* (Romans 8:1)? Have you ever heard better news? This truth should encourage us to know the Lord as intimately as possible: To pant after Him *"As the deer pants for the water brooks..."* (Psalm 42:1). One thing is certain: The more we know Him, the more we will love Him. The more we love Him, the more we will desire to glorify Him through every thought and deed. No wonder Paul writes:

> *...we are under obligation, not to the flesh, to live according to the flesh—*
> (Romans 8:12)

After all that God has done for us, we should realize that we are not obligated *"to live according to the flesh."* As we discovered last week, to *"walk according to the flesh"* means that we have allowed ungodly habit patterns stored in the brain, the brain being a piece of *"flesh,"* to influence our behavior. We do so when we believe the power of sin's lies sent into our minds by means of these ungodly patterns. Thus the phrases, *"live according to the flesh"* (Romans 8:12) and *"walk according to the flesh"* (Romans 8:4), are equivalent. Many of these ungodly habits were formed before we met Christ, but some are fashioned <u>after</u> we become believers. Yes, new sinful patterns are produced when I, the new self (the new man), believe the power of sin's lie in a new area and respond accordingly. Therefore, when I sin, it is the new self who has sinned, since I am the new self.

> *When I sin, it is the new self who has sinned, since I am the new self.*

To live *"according to the flesh"* means that we *"must die"* (Romans 8:13). Indeed, if we live *"according to the flesh"* long enough and don't experience physical death, we find ourselves living as though we are dead. In fact, to live in a prolonged state of disobedience, after having known the peace and joy of fellowship with Christ, results in nothing but defeat and despair. Joy and peace are restored through repentance and confession, but consequence is reaped from our disobedience the remainder of our stay on earth (Colossians 3:25). Yet, not once does God condemn us (Romans 8:1)!

Paul continues by writing:

> *...but if by the Spirit you are putting to death the deeds of the body, you will live.*
> (Romans 8:13)

Truth is amazing in that it exposes and incapacitates deception. As we yield to the *"Spirit"* of God (the *"Spirit"* of Truth), the power of sin which dwells in our physical body is defeated as it attempts to deceive us into being influenced by our ungodly habit patterns (reference Circle Diagram 8). It is through responding to the Spirit's prompting that we really *"live"*!

With this fact in mind, consider the following: Jesus was born void of a sin nature (old self) because he was the Father's Son, not the son of Joseph. On occasion, however, His mind was flooded with thoughts (lies) from Satan, as verified by Matthew 4:1-11. He chose to reject these thoughts (lies) the moment they entered and remained pure and holy. Jesus proves, therefore, that <u>a sinful thought does not result in sin until we allow it to negatively impact our thinking and, in turn, our behavior.</u> Consequently, we must refuse any thought that violates the principles taught in the full counsel of God's Word.

Are you developing a greater appreciation for truth? Doesn't this wonderful news encourage you to devour God's Word, to make it *"the joy"* of your *"heart"* (Psalm 119:111)? No doubt, the truth found in God alone will set us free from anything the enemy sends our way.

Sons Not Slaves

Paul teaches:

> *For all who are being led by the Spirit of God, these are sons of God.* (Romans 8:14)

If a man is being *"led by the Spirit"* on a fairly consistent basis, he shows himself to be a son *"of God."* No one, not even the greatest of saints, is *"led by the Spirit"* every moment of the day. Thus, if we are open to the Spirit's leading, it confirms that we are believers.

We become *"sons of God,"* and receive the Holy *"Spirit,"* at the point of justification (salvation). But we must learn to be *"led by the Spirit."* We are being *"led by the Spirit"* when we allow the thoughts directed into our minds by means of the *"Spirit"* to control our lives, thoughts that are always in agreement with the Word of God. *"The Spirit"* grants wisdom to make proper choices, which in turn frees us to live as Jesus lived. After all, He taught that *"the Spirit"* is *"the Spirit of truth"* and that He would *"guide"* us *"into all the truth"* (John 16:13).

We are given even more encouraging news in Romans 8:15:

> *For you have not received a spirit of slavery leading to fear again, but you have received a spirit of adoption as sons by which we cry out, "Abba! Father!"*
> (Romans 8:15)

Paul states that we *"...have not received a spirit of slavery leading to fear again,"* but *"a spirit of adoption as sons by which we cry out, 'Abba! Father!'"* No doubt, the *"spirit of adoption"* we have *"received"* frees us to perceive God as a loving *"Father"* Who has our best interests in mind. Simply put, if we are justified (saved), we are sons of God whether we <u>feel</u> like it or not. We must communicate these wonderful truths to all who will listen, for an improper view of the Father keeps many from accepting Christ as Savior.

The *"Spirit"* reveals to us *"that we are children of God,"* and He does so through bearing *"witness with our spirit"* (Romans 8:16). No need to be afraid of God, for He is our Father. We are also *"...heirs of God and fellow heirs with Christ..."* (Romans 8:17). In fact, when *"all things"* are summed up *"in Christ"* (Ephesians 1:10), we will be *"fellow heirs with"* Him (Romans 8:17)—possessing all that He possesses. We are also *"heirs of God"* (v.17), confirming that we are His offspring and *"heirs"* of everything He has to bestow. What could possibly keep us from becoming legitimate bond-servants of this God Who loves us so?

*H**e builds character in the fiber of our being through using the difficulties of life for our good— the only thing that will prepare us to reign.*

The last phrase of Romans 8:17 must not be overlooked. Do you realize that as a result of being *"heirs of God and fellow heirs with Christ,"* we will *"also be glorified with Him"*? According to Revelation 3:21 and Revelation 20:4, we will rule with Him as well. Consequently, God must train us for such a responsible position. How does He do so? He builds character in the fiber of our being through using the difficulties of life for our good—the only thing that will prepare us to reign.

Hope in the Midst of Suffering

Paul's maturity allowed him to perceive his *"sufferings"* as unworthy *"to be compared with the glory that is to be revealed to us"* (Romans 8:18). This statement is extraordinary considering the extreme persecution he encountered while preaching the gospel. In fact, 2Corinthians 11 and 12 are required reading when our difficulties seem overwhelming. Paul was persecuted severely, but he considered his *"sufferings"* as nothing compared to *"the glory"* that would follow:

> *For momentary, light affliction is producing for us an eternal weight of glory far beyond all comparison, while we look not at the things which are seen, but at the things which are not seen; for the things which are seen are temporal, but the things which are not seen are eternal.* (2Corinthians 4:17-18)

Do you realize that *"...the whole creation groans and suffers..."* (Romans 8:22)? From the day that Adam sinned, *"creation"* has lived in pain. No wonder it is waiting for *"...the revealing of the sons of God..."* (v.19), an event that releases it *"...from its slavery..."* (v.21). In fact, Isaiah 30:23-26, Isaiah 35:1-2, and Ezekiel 36:28-38 describe the degree to which creation will be blessed when Christ returns with His bride, the church, at His Second Coming.

We *"groan"* as well (v.23). We who possess *"the first fruits of the Spirit...groan"* because we are *"waiting eagerly for our adoption as sons, the redemption of our body."* In other words, we "groan" because we live in bodies that will die, bodies that are now inhabited by the power of sin. We learned earlier in the course that the new self (the new man—the real us—our soul and spirit) is already redeemed, perfect, holy, blameless, etc. Our bodies are not yet redeemed, however, for they are mortal and will one day die! Think about this truth for a moment. At the point of physical death, our brains will die, and our ungodly habit patterns will become extinct. It is then that the power of sin will cease sending thoughts into our minds, thoughts that sometimes deceive us into believing that error is truth. Thus, only after our physical bodies die will we be perfected in our behavior.

> *At the point of physical death, our brains will die, and our ungodly habit patterns will become extinct.*

Our Adoption as Sons

Paul also confirms that the phrase *"our adoption as sons"* (v.23) points to *"the redemption of our body."*

> *...waiting eagerly for our adoption as sons, the redemption of our body.*
> (Romans 8:23)

This proves that the day we receive our glorified, immortal bodies will be the day we are adopted in the fullest sense. We will then be holy, perfect, blameless, etc. in spirit, soul, and body, not just in spirit and soul as we presently are. All church saints, the church beginning in Acts 2, will receive their glorified bodies at the Rapture of the church (1Thessalonians 4:13-17).

No doubt, our brains, which store our ungodly habit patterns, will vanish along with our physical bodies, since the brain is part of the body. In fact, we will receive new, immortal brains,

brains void of ungodly habit patterns. It is then that our behavior, exemplified through our new, immortal bodies, will line up with what we have been in our spirits and souls since the point of justification (salvation)! What an amazing, omnipotent, omniscient, wise, and loving God we serve!!!

Thinking through our Findings

Is your understanding being opened to the fact that God makes our souls and spirits holy and perfect at the point of justification, even though our behavior will not be perfected until after the death of our bodies? Take a few minutes to review the questions associated with the fourth day of Week 11. Are you seeing that our behavior is not who we are, but that who we are consists of what God makes our souls and spirits into at the point of justification (salvation)? Are you comprehending why we will continue to commit acts of sin so long as we are in our earthly bodies? Sinless perfection is impossible this side of heaven, yet many areas of weakness can be overcome through God's indwelling power within us. Yes, the ungodly habit patterns, stored in the brain, actually decrease in intensity as we mature in the faith. We must think long and hard on what we are addressing here, for it is the absolute key to victory.

Let's take what we gleaned from Romans 6:6 (Weeks 11 and 12) and attach it to our latest findings. Suppose, hypothetically, that the old self (sin nature) remains alive in a New Testament believer—that it was wounded but not eradicated when we were justified (saved). This false assumption would create a theological nightmare, for our

> *We must think long and hard on what we are addressing here, for it is the absolute key to victory.*

souls and spirits would be part evil and part holy under such an arrangement—the old self being evil and the new self being holy. How then could we enter into God's presence at the point of physical death? We couldn't!

Can you see the necessity of the old self being eradicated through God's act of justification? Physical death <u>cannot</u> remove the old self, for the old self is <u>not</u> part of the body. The old self is soul and spirit. It is who we were before we were saved, for we receive a new soul and spirit at the point of justification. Only the cross is capable of eradicating who we used to be, for *"our old self was crucified with"* Christ (Romans 6:6). Thus, it is imperative that the *"old self"* be eradicated at the point of justification rather than when we succumb to physical death.

Saved by Hope

Certainly, *"...in hope we have been saved..."* (Romans 8:24-25). *"Hope"* provides incentive to *"wait"* for what God has promised, in fact, to *"wait"* for the unseen. *"Hope"* is born through realizing that our present suffering will one day be exchanged for glory beyond our ability to currently comprehend. *"The first fruits of the Spirit,"* which we now possess as believers (v.23), allow us to live in this perspective. Consequently, the remedy to current suffering is a proper view of the *"unseen"* (2 Corinthians 4:17-18; Hebrews 11:27). No wonder, Paul wrote, *"Set your mind on the things above, and not on the things that are on the earth"* (Colossians 3:2); for *"...our citizenship is in heaven"* (Philippians 3:20); and it is from this vantage point that we are to view *"the things"* that touch our lives.

Only one more week, and you will have completed the course. You are growing, so be encouraged!

Romans 8:26-39 Questions

First Day

1. Remember to pray for wisdom. Read Romans 8:1-39. How does *"the Spirit"* assist us when we *"pray"* (vv.26-27)?

2. What does Paul say about *"the Spirit"* in 1Corinthians 2:11-12?

3. Of the different truths you studied today regarding *"the Spirit,"* what encouraged you the most, and why?

4. Attempt to find additional New Testament verses that address the function of *"the Spirit"* in the life of a New Testament believer.

Second Day

1. Read Romans 8:26-39. What does Romans 8:28 communicate to you?

2. If all church saints viewed life from the perspective mentioned in verse 28, what would occur in the body of Christ?

3. List at least two instances where God took a very difficult situation and used it for your good.

4. What keeps you from viewing all adversity through the eyes of Romans 8:28?

5. Why could Paul teach verse 28 with such authority?

Third Day

1. Read Romans 8:26-39. After reading Romans 8:29, how would you define the words *"foreknew"* and *"predestined"*?

2. According to Romans 8:30, God does several things for the person who is *"predestined."* List them.

3. Paul writes that God has *"glorified"* New Testament believers in the here and now (v.30)? What does he mean? Considering your answer, what portion of your three-part-being (spirit, soul, and body) has already been *"glorified"*? Based on passages such as 1 Thessalonians 4:16-17, when will you receive your glorified body? This week's lesson will assist you should you have difficulty answering today's questions.

Fourth Day

1. Read Romans 8:26-39. Why is Romans 8:31 such a powerful statement to those who know Christ?

2. The word *"give"* (v.32) is in the future tense, meaning that God would supply every future need of the believers at Rome. The same support applies to us as well. Now that you are a believer, do you perceive your daily blessings (*"Every good thing...and every perfect gift..."*— James 1:17) as coming forth from God? Do you thank the Lord regularly for His many gifts? If not, what prevents you from doing so?

3. Why can no one *"...bring a charge against God's elect..."* (v.33)? How would you define the word *"elect"*?

4.   Why can no one condemn a New Testament believer (v.34)? How does this principle tie in with Romans 8:1?

Fifth Day

1.   Read Romans 8:26-39. Read verses 35-39 a second time and enjoy the good news recorded there. Write down some of the thoughts that came to mind as you read these passages.

2.   If we constantly live by the principles taught in verses 35-39, what changes will occur in our lives?

3.   When did you last use these verses in the midst of a difficult situation?

Sixth Day

1.   What is the most significant truth you learned in this study?

2.   Have the truths of Romans 1-8 encouraged you to know Jesus more intimately? If so, why?

3.   Do you desire that others know what you now know regarding Romans 1-8? Could you explain what you have gleaned to someone else?   If you are interested in digging deeper, we have weekend conferences for that purpose. For details, contact us at The Hill, P.O. Box 13, Hardin, Ky. 42048, or access our website at www.lifeonthehill.org. Our phone number is 270-437-4172.

Romans 8:26-39 Lesson

The Intercession of the Spirit

Have you ever needed to pray, but couldn't? You try to say the words, but they just won't come. Or have you prayed and felt like your words were meaningless and empty? If so, great news is on the horizon! Paul says that during these times, in fact at all times when we pray, *"...the Spirit Himself intercedes for us with groanings too deep for words"* (Romans 8:26). Paul then states that *"...the Spirit...intercedes for the saints according to the will of God"* (Romans 8:27). Thus, when we pray, *"the Spirit...intercedes for us"* according to the Father's perfect plan. Wonderful!

It is startling that Paul viewed himself as incapable of praying as he should (notice his use of *"we"* in verse 26). Knowing Paul's thoughts encourages me greatly, for I doubt if any of us are totally satisfied with the depth of our communication with God.

Paul writes more regarding *"the Spirit"* in 1Corinthians 2:11-12:

> *For who among men knows the thoughts of a man except the spirit of the man, which is in him? Even so the thoughts of God no one knows except the Spirit of God. Now we have received, not the spirit of the world, but the Spirit who is from God, that we might know the things freely given to us by God,* (1Corinthians 2:11-12)

Paul states that *"the Spirit...knows...the thoughts of God."* He also writes that *"the Spirit"* was given *"that we might know the things freely given to us by God."* Yes, the Holy *"Spirit"* not only leads us into a deeper understanding of God's heart, but reveals what He (God) has *"freely given"* to all New Testament believers subsequent to their exercising repentance and faith while depraved. No wonder Paul writes:

> *For to us God revealed them through the Spirit; for the Spirit searches all things, even the depths of God.* (1Corinthians 2:10)

All for Good

What if you knew beyond doubt that God is capable of using everything that crosses your path, in fact, everything that occurs in space and time, *"for* [your] *good"?* Paul teaches this wonderful truth in Romans 8:28, truth relating to *"...those who are called according to His purpose."* Would worry or anxiety hold a place in your life should you adopt such a mindset? No way! You would perceive God as totally sovereign, freeing you to live and relax in a state of *"rest"* (Hebrews 4:9). Can you imagine how the world would view believers should the body of Christ embrace this truth?

God's Foreknowledge

God has given man a free will to choose as he pleases, but God knows beforehand what choices he will make. Thus, God possesses foreknowledge.

Do you realize that God knows, and has always known, everything that will transpire in the future? God has given man a free will to choose as he pleases, but God knows beforehand what choices he will make (Psalm 139:1-4). Thus, God possesses foreknowledge. It is essential that we understand this fact, for in Romans 8:29 Paul declares:

> *For whom He foreknew, He also predestined to become conformed to the image of His Son...* (Romans 8:29)

We must exercise caution here, for some perceive this passage as teaching that God determines who will or won't be saved—that God seals our destiny before we are born. They believe that a person must be elected to salvation from eternity past if he is to be saved at some point after physical birth. Is this a proper view of Paul's words, or is he communicating something totally different?

As previously expressed, God possesses foreknowledge. He knows, and has always known, everything that has occurred, is occurring, or will occur from eternity past through eternity future. In fact, all that transpires from eternity past through eternity future is constantly before Him. Consequently, it is not required that God cause all things to know all things, as some have incorrectly assumed. Their incorrect assumptions force them to redefine *"foreknew"* (Romans 8:29) as "foreordained" or "predestined," which is totally unfair to the text.

Terms can't be manipulated, changed, or redefined in an attempt to validate an unscriptural experience or contradictory system of thought. In fact, we are never to allow an experience or system of thought to dictate what we accept or reject regarding God's infallible Word. Rather, we are to always allow God's Word to dictate what we accept or reject regarding all experiences or systems of thought! Scripture is never to be at the mercy of a particular way of thinking. Instead, all ways of thinking are to be at the mercy of the Scriptures. Changing the definition or meaning of the terms used in God's holy Word is an indictment against the God who composed it. This manipulation must never be allowed—no matter who views it as proper.

Scripture is never to be at the mercy of a particular way of thinking. Instead, all ways of thinking are to be at the mercy of the Scriptures.

Predestination

Everyone has a free will and can, in the midst of their depravity, accept or reject Christ (John 1:12, Acts 16:31, Acts 26:18, Romans 10:9-10, and hoard of additional verses). Once we exercise repentance and faith while depraved and are placed in Christ through the power of the Holy Spirit (1Corinthians 12:13), we are *"predestined"* (Romans 8:29). To what are we *"predestined"* once we are in Jesus? We are *"...predestined to become conformed to the image of His [God's] Son..."* (Romans 8:29), a conformity that includes receiving a resurrected body at the Rapture of the church. This truth will be confirmed by interpreting Scripture in context, so we will begin by revisiting Romans 8:29 and build from there.

The phrase, *"that He might be the first-born among many brethren"* (Romans 8:29), is powerfully interesting. But for proper interpretation we must note its relationship to the previous phrases in the passage:

> *For whom He foreknew, He also predestined to become conformed to the image of His Son, that He might be the first-born among many brethren;* (Romans 8:29)

Jesus is *"the first-born"* of the Father in the sense that He was the first to receive a resurrected body. Colossians 1:18 validates this fact:

...and He is the beginning, the first-born from the dead...(Colossians 1:18)

If Jesus is described as *"the first-born"* of the Father due to His bodily resurrection (Colossians 1:18), then Romans 8:29 must point, not only to Jesus' bodily resurrection, but also to the future bodily resurrection of all New Testament believers:

...that He might be the first-born among many brethren; (Romans 8:29)

*G*od *"predestined" us (after we exercised repentance and faith while depraved) to receive a glorified body at the Rapture of the church.*

The fact that we are part of the *"many brethren"* confirms that God *"predestined"* us (after we exercised repentance and faith while depraved) to receive a glorified body at the Rapture of the church. Many blessings accompany this wonderful event. Consequently, church saints will live throughout the Millennium and the Eternal Order in a glorified body, responding properly to the variables placed before them. Why? Each church saint will live in a body, not only void of the old brain, which houses sinful habit patterns (and godly habit patterns as well), but a body void of the power of sin, a power which lives in the <u>body</u> of every believer (and unbeliever as well) during his stay on the earth (Romans 7:23). No doubt, the New Testament believer has been given a glorious future destiny—that of receiving a glorified body at the Rapture of the church.

This truth ties in perfectly with 1Corinthians 15:51-55:

> *...we shall not all sleep, but we shall all be changed, in a moment, in the twinkling of an eye, at the last trumpet; for the trumpet will sound, and the dead will be raised imperishable, and we shall be changed. For this perishable must put on the imperishable, and this mortal must put on immortality. But when this perishable will have put on the imperishable, and this mortal will have put on immortality, then will come about the saying that is written, "DEATH IS SWALLOWED UP in victory. "O DEATH, WHERE IS YOUR VICTORY? O DEATH, WHERE IS YOUR STING?"* (1Corinthians 15:51-55)

Be sure to realize that the resurrection addressed in 1Corinthians 15:51-55 is different from Lazarus' experience in John 11. Lazarus was raised back to natural life, back to mortal life, meaning that his body would die a second time. The same principle applies to all who are raised back to natural life, such as Tabitha in Acts 9:36-43. Jesus' body, on the other hand, was resurrected to immortal life, never to die again. Thus, in conjunction with our souls and spirits being placed in Christ (subsequent to repenting and believing while depraved), we were predestined to receive a glorified body so we, at the Rapture of the church, can be a recipient of this same immortal life.

Note: When a New Testament believer dies, his soul and spirit eject out of the earthly body and instantaneously enter heaven (2Corinthians 5:8), while the physical body returns to dust. At the Rapture, the church saint's soul and spirit will be joined to his resurrected body for all eternity (1Thessalonians 4:13-18).

Romans 8:23 teaches the same truth regarding predestination when linked with Ephesians 1:5:

> *And not only this, but also we ourselves, having the first fruits of the Spirit, even we ourselves groan within ourselves, waiting eagerly for <u>our adoption as sons,</u> <u>the redemption of our body.</u>* (Romans 8:23)

The phrase, *"our adoption as sons,"* points to *"the redemption of the body"* (Romans 8:23)—that moment in the future when we receive our resurrected, glorified, immortal bodies. According to Ephesians 1:5, we have been *"predestined"* to this—*"to adoption as sons"*.

> *He <u>predestined us to adoption as sons</u> through Jesus Christ to Himself,*
> *according to the kind intention of His will,* (Ephesians 1:5)

This verse confirms that New Testament believers are *"predestined"* to receive glorified bodies—not predestined to be saved. When, then, are they *"predestined"*? They are *"predestined"* in conjunction with being placed in Christ subsequent to exercising repentance and faith while depraved. Consequently, if you are a believer, you were *"predestined"* the moment you were saved, meaning that your future destiny is this: You will one day receive a glorified body and experience all the benefits associated with that wonderful transformation.

Thus, the word *"predestined"* (Romans 8:29) can be summed up in the following statement:

> We were <u>not</u> predestined to be saved from eternity past by means of an eternal
> decree of God. Rather, in conjunction with being saved (justified) through being
> placed in Christ subsequent to exercising our own personal repentance and faith
> while depraved, we received a glorious future destiny—that of one day living in a
> glorified body.

Predestination has to do with believers only, for we were *"predestined"* when God made us new. Therefore, predestination has nothing to do with who will or will not be saved, but has everything to do with the New Testament believer receiving a glorified body at the Rapture of the church. Because the Father possesses foreknowledge, He knows who will choose (while depraved) to accept Christ and receive this glorious future destiny—foreknowledge meaning "to know beforehand." He also knows who will reject Christ's free offer of salvation and the resulting blessings. Consequently, foreknowledge means "foreknowledge." It cannot be redefined as foreordain or predestine, as some have erroneously assumed.

> *P*redestination has nothing to do
> with who will or will not be saved,
> but has everything to do with the
> New Testament believer receiving
> a glorified body at the Rapture of
> the church.

Isn't predestination simple when studied in context? New Testament believers are predestined (once they are placed in Christ subsequent to repenting and believing while depraved) to receive a glorified body at the Rapture of the church. What is complicated about that? Nothing is complicated about that! It is the contradictory systems of thought that have brought the confusion. For more input, you can obtain a copy of *God's Heart: As it Relates to Foreknowledge/Predestination* distributed by this ministry.

More Wonderful News

Paul also teaches that those *"whom He predestined...He also called"* (named or gave a role or position in the body of Christ), *"justified"* (made not guilty before Him—as we studied in Romans 5:1), and *"glorified"* (v.30). Note that the action associated with *"predestined,"* *"called,"* *"justified,"* and *"glorified"* is past tense action, meaning that if you are a believer, you are already *"predestined,"* *"called,"* *"justified,"* and *"glorified."*

The past tense in regard to *"glorified"* verifies that God sees our spirits and souls, who we are, as finished products. You may ask, "Doesn't Philippians 3:21 teach that Jesus *'...will transform the body of our humble state into conformity with the body of His glory...,'* and doesn't this transpire at some point after we are released from our earthly body?" No doubt, you will receive your glorified body at some point in the future. But the term *"glorified"* in Romans 8:30 is not referencing this wonderful event. *"Glorified"* in this context points to what was done in our spirits and souls in conjunction with being placed in Christ and made new—after repenting and believing while depraved. Consequently, when we were placed in Christ, subsequent to our exercising repentance and faith while depraved, our spirits and souls were *"glorified"* to the greatest degree possible—in an instant of time! (Review the lesson from Week 7.) Yes, we will commit acts of sin so long as we live in our physical bodies. But even in the midst of these sinful acts, we are *"glorified"* saints who have made temporary mistakes, not lowly second-class citizens of the kingdom. Remember that when we sin, it is the new man who has sinned.

God's Awesome Provision and Protection

Do you have enemies who attempt to disrupt what God is doing in and through you? If so, Paul has the answer to your dilemma. He says, *"...If God is for us, who is against us"* (v.31). He then adds that God will *"...freely give us all things"* (v.32), meaning that He will abundantly supply all future needs. Paul follows in verses 33 and 34 by declaring that no one can *"...bring a charge against God's elect..."* Why is this so? *"...God is the one who justifies"* (Romans 8:33; Romans 5:1). Because Jesus died, rose, and assumed an intercessory role for us in heaven, we cannot be condemned. Yes, God is in our corner and rooting for us. Truly, He is our friend?

Do you at times question God's love? Should you face pain and hardship, does it mean that God no longer cares for you? Paul was equipped to answer questions of this sort, as verified by Romans 8:35-39. After intense trial and persecution, he still writes:

*G**od sees our spirits and souls, who we are, as finished products.*

> But in all these things we overwhelmingly conquer through Him who loved us.
> (Romans 8:37)

He realized that Christ's indwelling presence could conquer any hardship, for Christ was his *"life"* (Colossians 3:4). However, to understand the significance of Christ's presence in our lives, suffering is normally required. In fact, pain allows us to say with Paul: *"...neither death, nor life, nor angels, nor principalities, nor things present, nor things to come, nor powers, nor height, nor depth, nor any other created thing, shall be able to separate us from the love of God, which is in Christ Jesus our Lord."* (Romans 8:38-39)

Are you yet *"convinced"* (v.38)? If not, you can rest assured that God knows what it will take for this change of heart to occur. Due to His unfathomable love, He is absolutely determined that you learn to live from His perspective—the only perspective that provides hope in the midst of a society inundated with chaos, turmoil, and despair.

May God bless you, and may He use what we have studied to transform your life and the lives of those around you. Take every opportunity to know our Lord as intimately as possible. You will then stand amazed as He, through your unique personality, enriches and deepens the lives of those seeking the most excellent way.

Think on the things you have heard. Several who have studied with us have returned months and even years later and said, "I am finally understanding how to apply what I learned in Romans 1-8. It took some challenging circumstances to bring it about, but the Lord knew what I needed, and I am thankful."

It is the Lord's responsibility to mature you as you face the variables of life. Therefore, take hold of His huge, powerful hand and let Him lead you through the sunshine and the rain, realizing every step of the way that He is working it all for your good!

Shalom.

Note: An advanced version of this study *(Advancing in Romans: From Faith to Faith)* is available should you desire to dig deeper. It takes the foundational course you have completed, however, to prepare you for the depth of that subject matter. Now that you are prepared, please feel free to get in touch with us should you be interested at www.lifeonthehill.org or call 270-437-4172.

Diagram 1

Man is a Three Part Being
1Thessalonians 5:23

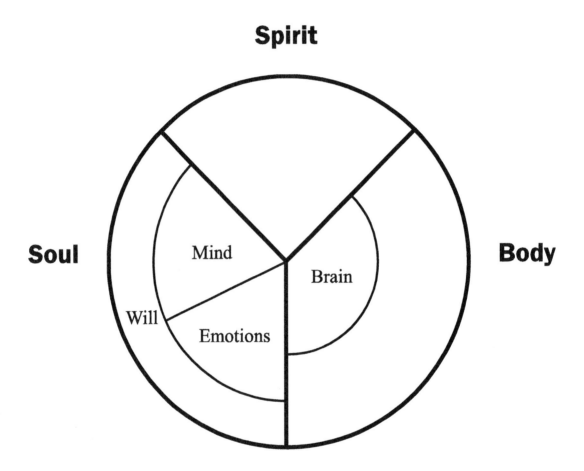

Now may the God of peace Himself sanctify you entirely; and may your spirit and soul and body be preserved complete without blame at the coming of our Lord Jesus Christ, (1Thessalonians 5:23)

Body: What houses the soul and spirit (2Corinthians 5:1-4). Notice that the brain is part of the body.

Soul: Mind, Emotions and Will. Man thinks with his mind, feels with his emotions, and chooses with his will.

Spirit: The part of a New Testament believer that house's God's presence (John 14:16-17, 20, 23). Void of God's presence, this part of man is dead to God (Genesis 2:17; Ephesians 2:1). It is through the avenue of the Spirit that man communicates with God (John 4:24), and God with man (John 14:26).

Diagram 2

Sin (the Power of Sin) Entered into Man

Romans 5:12

Just as through one man sin entered into the world, and death through sin, and so death spread to all men because all sinned, (Romans 5:12)

When Adam disobeyed God, the law of sin (the power of sin, sin) moved into Adam's spirit, soul, and body. Adam was then influenced by the messages he received from the law of sin (the power of sin, sin).

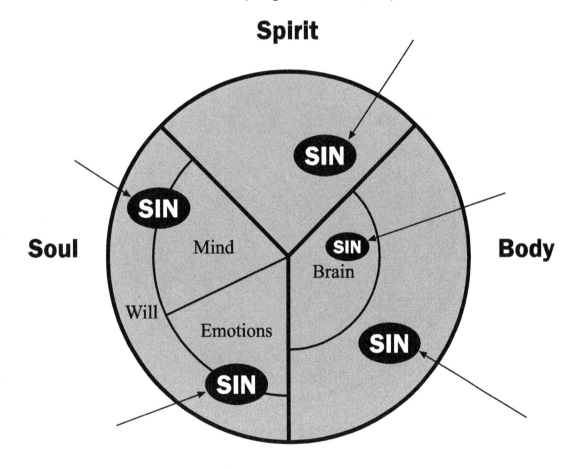

Diagram 3

Man without Christ
Romans 5:12

When Adam sinned the Adamic Nature was born, the Adamic Nature being soul and spirit. It was then natural for Adam to be controlled by the Power of Sin that lived in his spirit, soul, and body.

Man is born in the same condition that Adam was in after he sinned. Man is born spiritually separated from God, but not to the degree that he is incapable of exercising personal repentance and faith while depraved. The Power of Sin generates ungodly thoughts that the depraved generally accept as the truth.

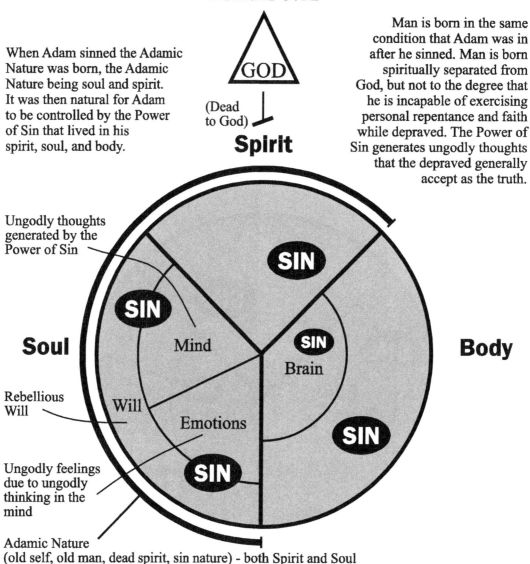

Ungodly thoughts generated by the Power of Sin

Rebellious Will

Ungodly feelings due to ungodly thinking in the mind

Adamic Nature (old self, old man, dead spirit, sin nature) - both Spirit and Soul
Also refer to circle Diagram 9.

Just as through one man sin entered into the world, and death through sin, and so death spread to all men because all sinned, (Romans 5:12)

The terms old self, old man, dead spirit, sin nature, and Adamic Nature (listed above as the spirit and soul of lost mankind) are all synonymous. When you see one of these terms, either in the course or in Scripture, know that it refers to the nature that Adam possessed after he sinned. Since we are descendants of Adam, we are born with this same nature. This nature is rebellious toward God, but not so much so that it can't repent and exercise faith.

Make sure that you don't confuse the sinful nature with the power of sin (sin). They are different in that the sinful nature has to do with the nature of lost mankind, while the power of sin (sin) is Satan's messenger (Satan's agent).

Diagram 4

Man with Christ
2Corinthians 5:17

The Old Self
The Adamic Nature (old self, old man, dead spirit, sin nature) is crucified and eradicated the moment we repent and believe while depraved. It is crucified with Christ (Romans 6:6).

The Spirit is <u>Alive</u> to God
The Power of Sin is expelled from the spirit and soul of the New Testament believer when salvation occurs. It remains, however, in the body.

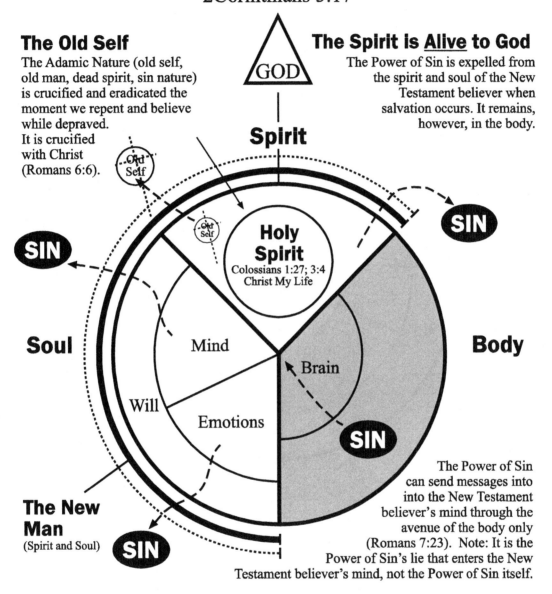

The Power of Sin can send messages into into the New Testament believer's mind through the avenue of the body only (Romans 7:23). Note: It is the Power of Sin's lie that enters the New Testament believer's mind, not the Power of Sin itself.

... Christ in you, the hope of glory. (Colossians 1:27)

When Christ, who is our life,... (Colossians 3:4)

Therefore if any man is in Christ, he is a new creature; the old things passed away; behold new things have come. (2Corinthians 5:17)

Knowing this, that our old self was crucified with Him,... (Romans 6:6)

...greater is He who is in you than he who is in the world. (1 John 4:4)

But I see a different law in the members of my body, waging war against the law of my mind, and making me a prisoner of the law of sin which is in my members. (Romans 7:23)

Diagram 5

How We Operate

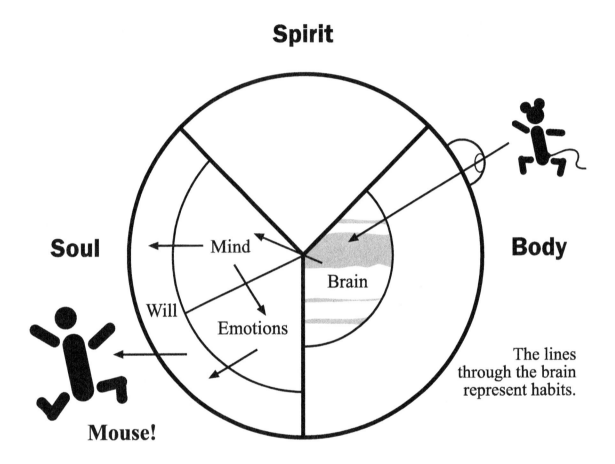

Diagram 6

How the Power of Sin is Defeated

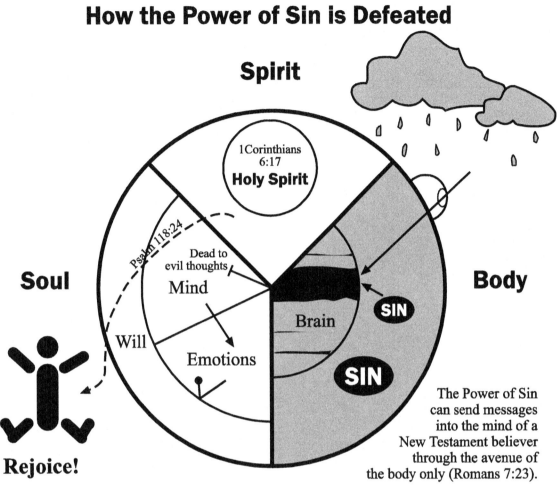

The Power of Sin can send messages into the mind of a New Testament believer through the avenue of the body only (Romans 7:23).

Rejoice!

My mind is no longer enslaved to evil thoughts. My new spirit and the Holy Spirit are one. Therefore, I can consistently respond to the truth ushered into my mind through the power of the Holy Spirit and walk in victory.

> *But the one who joins himself to the Lord is one spirit with Him.* (1Corinthians 6:17)

> *This is the day which the Lord has made; Let us rejoice and be glad in it.* (Psalm 118:24)

All our habits (good and bad) are stored in the brain, and our brain is part of our physical body. While living in our lost condition, we developed many ungodly habits. We also develop ungodly habits after we become believers. We do so by repeatedly yielding to the Power of Sin's lie in a particular area of our lives. Satan's messenger (the Power of Sin) sends sinful thoughts into our minds through the avenue of these ungodly habit patterns (Romans 7:17, 20, and 23). It does so for two reasons: (1) To make us think that we generate the sinful thoughts entering our minds (2) To attempt to trick us into believing that the old man is still alive.

Note: Those ungodly habit patterns are reduced in size (intensity) as we mature in the Lord and learn to walk by His Spirit.

Diagram 7

Sin in Control
Romans 6:12

Walking (or Living) According to the Flesh
Romans 8:4-5

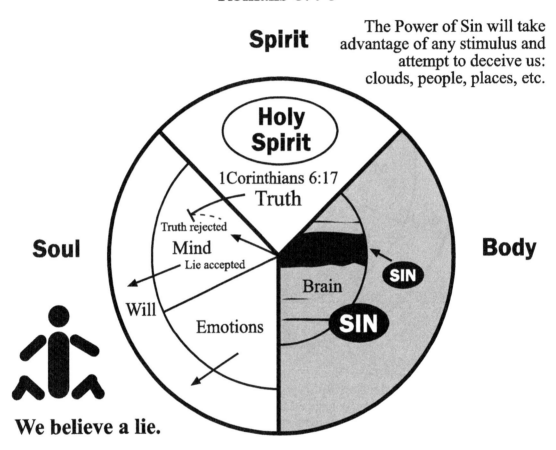

Spirit

The Power of Sin will take advantage of any stimulus and attempt to deceive us: clouds, people, places, etc.

Soul

Body

We believe a lie.

When we walk according to the flesh, we have failed to consider ourselves dead to the lie that the Power of Sin has sent into our minds (Romans 6:11). We have also failed to respond to the truth that the Spirit of God has sent in our minds. Thus, when this occurs, the new man sins.

> *Therefore do not let sin reign in your mortal body that you should obey its lusts,* (Romans 6:12)
>
> *in order that the requirement of the Law might be fulfilled in us, who do not walk according to the flesh, but according to the Spirit. For those who are according to the flesh set their minds on the things of the flesh, but those who are according to the Spirit, the things of the Spirit.* (Romans 8:4-5)

When we walk according to the flesh, we have believed the Power of Sin's lie and walked according to one of our ungodly habit patterns stored in our brain (the brain being a piece of flesh).

Diagram 8

Spirit in Control
Romans 6:13

Walking (or Living) According to the Spirit
Romans 8:4-5

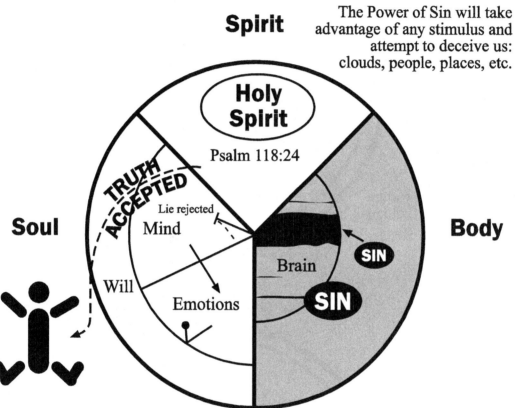

Spirit

The Power of Sin will take advantage of any stimulus and attempt to deceive us: clouds, people, places, etc.

We <u>do not</u> believe a lie!

My mind is no longer enslaved to the evil thoughts generated by the Power of Sin. My new spirit and the Holy Spirit are one (1Corinthians 6:17).

When we walk according to the Spirit, we have considered ourselves dead to the lie that the Power of Sin has sent into our minds (Romans 6:11). We have also responded to the truth that the Spirit of God has sent into our minds and, thus, have not allowed the Power of Sin to reign (Romans 6:12).

> *And do not go on presenting the members of your body to sin as instruments of unrighteousness; but present yourselves to God as those alive from the dead, and your members as instruments of righteousness to God. (Romans 6:13)*

> *in order that the requirement of the Law might be fulfilled in us, who do not walk according the flesh, but according to the Spirit. For those who are according to the flesh set their minds on the things of the flesh, but those who are according to the Spirit, the things of the Spirit. (Romans 8:4-5)*

Diagram 9   **The Old Self was Soul and Spirit**

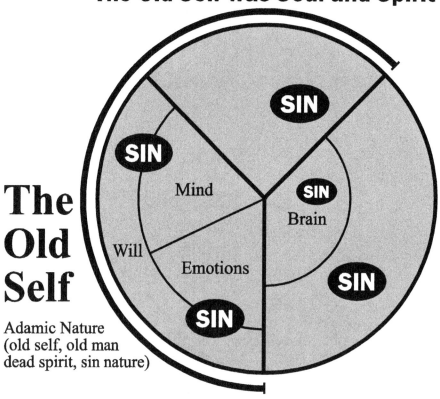

The Old Self

Adamic Nature
(old self, old man
dead spirit, sin nature)

The New Self is Soul and Spirit

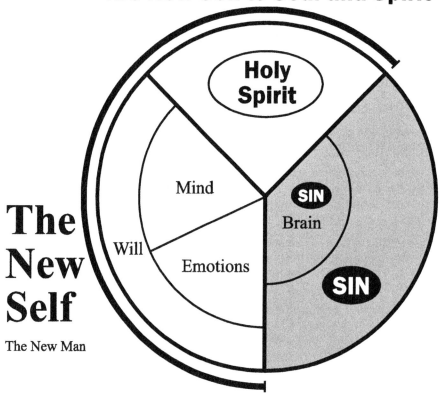

The New Self

The New Man

Romans 1-8 Course
Scripture Index
Scripture — page number

Genesis
1:1 — 39
2 — 64
2:16-17 — 106
2:17 — 66, 67
2:21-25 — 69
3 — 64, 66
3:6-7 — 66
3:7 — 48, 106
3:15 — 17
4 — 66
11:26-32 — 28
12:1-15:21 — 32
12:1 — 32
12:1-5 — 34
12:10-20 — 34
13:15 — 18
15 — 33
15:6 — 18, 28, 34, 35, 41
15:18 — 18
16 — 34
16:1 — 32
16:16 — 35
17:4-6 — 39
17:8 — 18
17:9-27 — 34, 35
17:19 — 34
17:22-24 — 33
17:24 — 18, 34, 35
19:1-11 — 6
19:12-26 — 6
19:38 — 32
20 — 34
20:1 — 32
22:1-19 — 34
20:12 — 34
22:17 — 39
22:24 — 32

Exodus
3:2 — 26, 29
13:21-22 — 26, 29
19:16-18 — 26, 29
20 — 9, 28, 39
20:18-21 — 19, 23
21:1-6 — 4
21:5-6 — 7

34:27-35 — 19, 23
40:34 — 26
40:34-38 — 29

Leviticus
17:11 — 62

Deuteronomy
15:12-17 — 4, 7

2Kings
22-23 — 23

1Chronicles
17:10-14 — 4
17:11-14 — 7

2Chronicles
5:13-14 — 26, 29
16:9 — 57

Psalms
22 — 7
42:1 — 119
118:24 — 94
119:111 — 120
139:1-4 — 126
145-150 — 38, 40

Proverbs
9:10 — 6

Ecclesiastes
4:9-12 — 2

Isaiah
26:3 — 56
30:23-26 — 118, 121
35:1-2 — 118, 121
40:31 — 56
53 — 7, 28

Ezekiel
11:22-25 — 26, 29
36:28-38 — 118, 121

Habakkuk
2:4 — 49

Matthew
2:3-6 — 22

4:1-11 — 119
4:3-11 — 93
6:12 — 86, 88 89
7:4-5 — 11
10:39 — 60, 62
23:37 — 51
26:17-18 — 59
27:20 — 22
27:35 — 59
27:50 — 59

Luke
2:8-9 — 26, 29
3:21-22 — 80
7:30 — 51
12:50 — 80
22:44 — 94
24:46-47 — 9

John
1:12 — 127
1:14 — 25, 26, 29
3:3-6 — 51, 74
3:19-21 — 62
4:24 — 66, 67, 74
6:44 — 50
8:37-39 — 34
11 — 128
15:12-13 — 60, 62
16:8 — 50
16:13 — 120

Acts
1:9 — 26, 29
1:11 — 7
2 — 40, 121
2:3 — 26, 29
5:29 — 52
5:31 — 52
7:37-38 — 19, 22
9:36-43 — 128
11:18 — 1, 11, 15, 34, 52, 69
16:31 — 18, 29, 50, 69, 127
26:18 — 50, 69, 127

Romans
1 — 4 10
1-3 — 62
1:1 — 98

[i] Dave Hunt, *What Love Is This?,* Third Edition, Published by the Berean Call, 2006, Page 425, Used by permission.

[ii] Wycliffe Bible Commentary, Edited by Charles F. Pfeiffer (OT) and Everett F. Harrison (NT), Copyright ©1962, 1990 The Moody Bible Institute of Chicago.

[iii] Vines Expository Dictionary of New Testament Words, By W. E. Vine, Merrill F. Unger, and William White Jr., Copyright ©1996 Thomas Nelson.

CPSIA information can be obtained at www.ICGtesting.com
Printed in the USA
BVOW09s1926210916

462895BV00005B/89/P